MW01006721

PHILOSOPHY AND ANIMAL LIFE

PHILOSOPHY AND ANIMAL LIFE

STANLEY CAVELL

CORA DIAMOND

JOHN MCDOWELL

IAN HACKING

AND CARY WOLFE

Columbia University Press New York

Columbia University Press
Publishers Since 1893
New York   Chichester, West Sussex

Introduction and conclusion copyright © 2008
Columbia University Press
Chapter 1 is reprinted with permission: Diamond, Cora, "The
Difficulty of Reality and the Difficulty of Philosophy," *Partial Answers*
1:2 (2003): 1–26 © Johns Hopkins University Press. Reprinted
with permission of The Johns Hopkins University Press.
Chapter 2 copyright © 2008 Stanley Cavell
Chapter 3 copyright © 2008 John McDowell

All rights reserved

Library of Congress Cataloging-in-Publication Data
Cavell, Stanley.
Philosophy and animal life / Stanley Cavell . . . [et al.].
p. cm.
Includes bibliographical references and index.
ISBN 978-0-231-14514-5 (cloth : alk. paper)
1. Animals (Philosophy) 2. Human-animal relationships. I. Title
B105.A55C38   2008
113'.8—dc22   2007046992

Columbia University Press books are printed on
permanent and durable acid-free paper.
This book is printed on paper with recycled content.
Printed in the United States of America
Designed by Audrey Smith

c 10 9 8 7 6 5 4 3 2 1

References to Internet Web sites (URLs) were
accurate at the time of writing. Neither the author nor
Columbia University Press is responsible for URLs that may have
expired or changed since the manuscript was prepared.

CONTENTS

PHILOSOPHY AND ANIMAL LIFE

INTRODUCTION

EXPOSURES

CARY WOLFE

In his novel *Disgrace*, J. M. Coetzee tells the story of David Lurie, a literature professor in South Africa whose career comes to an abrupt end after he has an affair with a female undergraduate and is charged with sexual harassment. Lurie moves to the country, where his daughter Lucy has a small farm, and begins volunteering at the local animal shelter, where he assists in euthanizing the scores of animals, mainly dogs, for whom no homes can be found. Lurie has never thought of himself as "a sentimentalist," as he puts it, and he takes to the work reluctantly. But then, gradually, he becomes absorbed in it.[1] "He had thought he would get used to it," Coetzee writes. "But that is not what happens. The more killings he assists in, the more jittery

1

he gets." Then, one Sunday night as he is driving back from the clinic, it hits him; "he actually has to stop at the roadside to recover himself. Tears flow down his face that he cannot stop; his hands shake. He does not understand what is happening to him." For reasons he doesn't understand, "his whole being is gripped by what happens in the [surgical] theatre" (143).

This moment in Coetzee's emotionally and politically complex novel is a kind of amplification of a passage from his contemporaneous work, *The Lives of Animals*, which serves as a touchstone in the essays that follow. In *The Lives of Animals*, the main character, novelist Elizabeth Costello, is haunted—"wounded," to use a figure that Cora Diamond highlights in "The Difficulty of Reality and the Difficulty of Philosophy"—by how we treat nonhuman animals in practices such as factory farming, a systemized and mechanized killing that she compares (to the consternation of some) in its scale and its violence to the Holocaust of the Jews during the Second World War. At a dinner after one of her invited public lectures, she is asked by the president of the university whether her vegetarianism "comes out of moral conviction," and she responds, against the expectations of her hosts, "No, I don't think so. . . . It comes out of a desire to save my soul." And when the university administrator politely replies, "Well, I have a great respect for it," she retorts impatiently, "I'm wearing leather shoes. I'm carrying a leather purse. I wouldn't have overmuch respect if I were you."[2]

What haunts Costello here, and what suddenly shakes David Lurie to his very soles as he is driving home that night, is the sheer weight and gravity of what has become one of the central ethical issues of our time: our moral responsibilities toward nonhuman animals. But both moments in Coetzee's work insist on something else, too, something that also, in a different way, unsettles the very foundations of what we call "the human," and in so doing reveals the characterization I just offered (of our responsibilities to animals as an "ethical issue") to be a kind of evasion of a problem that is not so easily disposed of. For both moments acknowledge a *second* kind of "unspeakability": not only the unspeakability of how we treat animals in practices such as factory farming but also the unspeakability of the limits of our own thinking in confronting such a reality—the trauma, as Diamond puts it, of "experiences in which we take something in reality to be resistant to our thinking it, or possibly to be painful in its inexplicability" ("The Difficulty of Reality," 45–46).

Writ large, in the terms of the (post-)Enlightenment philosophical tradition, this is often referred to as the problem of philosophical "skepticism," and part of what Diamond is interested in pressuring here is the extent to which the two questions that anchor this volume (philosophical skepticism and its consequences for ethics, and the question of our moral responsibilities to nonhuman animals)' are and are not versions of the same question. This is not to say that the papers collected here agree on this point; on the contrary, it seems to me that we find three rather different views on this matter—a situation that is brought into particularly sharp focus in John McDowell's response to both Cavell and Diamond and the extent to which Cavell's essay does justice to his own insights in this matter. For his part, Cavell has explored the question of skepticism with remarkable nuance and range over the past forty and more years. Working through figures as diverse as Kant, Descartes, Emerson, Wittgenstein, Austin, and Heidegger (among others), Cavell has plumbed the consequences of what it means to do philosophy in the wake of what he calls the Kantian "settlement" with skepticism. As he characterizes it in *In Quest of the Ordinary*, "To settle with skepticism . . . to assure us that we do know the existence of the world, or rather, that what we understand as knowledge is *of* the world, the price Kant asks us to pay is to cede any claim to know the thing in itself, to grant human knowledge is not of things as they are in themselves. You don't—do you?—have to be a romantic to feel sometimes about that settlement: Thanks for nothing."[3] But if, on Cavell's reading of Kant, "reason proves its power to itself, over itself" (30) by logically deriving the difference between the world of mere appearances (phenomena) that we can know and the world of the *Ding an sich* (noumena), which our knowledge never touches, then we find ourselves in a position that is not just odd but in fact profoundly unsettling, for philosophy in a fundamental sense then fails precisely insofar as it succeeds. We gain knowledge, but only to lose the world.

The question in the wake of skepticism thus becomes: What can it mean to (continue to) do philosophy after philosophy has become, in a certain sense, impossible? One thing it does *not* mean (if we believe the essays collected here) is that such "resistance" of the world ("the difficulty of reality," to use the phrase Diamond borrows from novelist John Updike) could be dissolved or overcome by ever-more ingenious or accomplished propositional arguments, ever-more refined philosophical concepts. Indeed, to think that it can—to mistake "the difficulty of philosophy" for the "difficulty of reality" (as Diamond suggests is the case with the philosophical "Reflections" published at the end of *The Lives of Animals*)—is to indulge in a "deflection" (to use Cavell's term) of a reality that impinges upon us—"befalls" us, as Wittgenstein once put it—in ways not masterable by the crafting of analytical arguments. (This is why, Diamond suggests, Elizabeth Costello does not offer an argument in defense of her vegetarianism, and it is also why Costello is quick to point to the inconsistency of her own practices with regard to animal products.) It is that impingement, that "pressure" of reality, that overtakes David Lurie on the drive back from the clinic. He literally does not know what is happening to him; he has no reasons for it and cannot explain it. And yet it is the most real thing in the world.

These fundamental challenges for (and to) philosophy are sounded by Cavell in his reading of the philosopher most important to him, Ralph Waldo Emerson, who writes in his most important essay, "Experience": "I take this evanescence and lubricity of all objects, which lets them slip through our fingers then when we clutch hardest, to be the most unhandsome part of our condition." For Cavell, this moment registers the confrontation with skepticism, certainly, but it also voices an understanding of how philosophy must change in the wake of that confrontation. For the "unhandsome" here names not just the Kantian *Ding an sich* but also, Cavell writes, "what happens when we seek to deny the stand-offishness of objects by clutching at them; which is to say, when we conceive thinking, say the application of concepts in judgments, as grasping something."[4] When we engage in that sort of "deflection," we only deepen the abyss—*"when we clutch hardest"*—between our thinking and the world that we want to understand. The opposite of clutching, on the other hand—what Cavell will call "the most handsome part of our condition"—is facing the fact that "the demand for unity in our judgments, that our deployment of concepts, is not the expression of the conditionedness or limitations of our humanness but of the human effort to escape our humanness" (*This New*, 86–87).

We may think that we have left the question of our relation to nonhuman animals behind at this juncture, but as both Cavell and Jacques Derrida remind us in their readings of Heidegger, the figure of the hand in relation to thought and to species difference is a linchpin of philosophical humanism. As Cavell points out, harbored in Heidegger's famous contention that "thinking is a handicraft" is the "fantasy of the apposable [*sic*] thumb" that separates the human from the animal not just anthropologically but also ontologically.[5] As Heidegger writes, in a moment emphasized by Derrida: "Apes, for example, have organs that can grasp, but they have no hand," for their being is subordinated to utility rather than devoted to thought and the reflection on things "as such," which is possible for only for beings who possess language.[6] Thus, the opposite of the "clutching" or "grasping" that will find its apotheosis for Heidegger in the world domination of technology is a thinking that is instead a kind of "reception" or welcoming (Cavell, *Conditions*, 39). Or as Derrida puts it, "If there is a thought of the hand or a hand of thought, as Heidegger gives us to think, it is not of the order of conceptual grasping. Rather this thought of the hand belongs to the essence of the *gift*, of a giving that would give, if this is possible, without taking hold of anything" ("*Geschlecht II*," 173). And thus Heidegger's insistence, as Cavell reminds us, on "the derivation of the word thinking from a root for thanking," as if "giving thanks for the gift of thinking" (*Conditions*, 39).

Philosophy can therefore no longer be seen as mastery, as a kind of clutching or grasping via analytical categories and concepts, which seemed, for Heidegger, "a kind of sublimized violence" (*Conditions*, 39). Rather, the duty of thinking is not to "deflect" but to receive and even suffer (remember Costello's woundedness) what Cavell calls our "exposure" to the world. That Diamond is much attracted to this term is clear not just because she begins her essay with a reading of a poem about a photograph but also because it underscores an important connection between the exposure of our concepts to the confrontation with skepticism and the *physical* exposure to vulnerability and mortality that we suffer because we, like animals, are embodied beings. As Diamond puts it in a key moment in her essay, unpacking her sense of Costello's startling assertion that "I know what it is like to be a corpse":

> The awareness we each have of being a living body, being "alive to the world", carries with it exposure to the bodily sense of vulnerability to death, sheer animal vulnerability, the vulnerability we share with them. This vulnerability is capable of panick-

ing us. To be able to acknowledge it at all, let alone as shared, is wounding; but acknowledging it as shared with other animals, in the presence of what we do to them, is capable not only of panicking one but also of isolating one, as Elizabeth Costello is isolated. Is there any difficulty in seeing why we should not prefer to return to moral debate, in which the livingness and death of animals enter as facts that we treat as relevant in this or that way, not as presences that may unseat our reason?

("The Difficulty of Reality," 74)

But there is yet a *third* type of exposure or finitude that is crucial here as well, as practiced readers of Heidegger (or, for that matter, of Cavell or Derrida) will have already guessed: our exposure—in a radical sense, our *subjection*—to language and writing in ways that bear very directly upon what it means to do philosophy, what philosophy *can* do in the face of these existential and ethical challenges. For one further consequence of everything I have been saying thus far is that the relationship between philosophical thinking ("concepts") and philosophy as a *writing* practice now takes on unprecedented importance (which is why Heidegger and Derrida and Cavell write the way they do—which is to say, "unphilosophically"). Against the backdrop of what is often referred to as the "linguistic turn" in twentieth-century philosophy, there is a direct line of connection between the problem of philosophical skepticism and the work of Wittgenstein on language, which will prove so important to all three of the philosophers collected here. But it is also on this point, as I will try to bring out later, that crucial differences emerge between this sort of work, emerging as it does out of an especially adventurous wing of the analytical tradition, and poststructuralist philosophy, particularly the work of Jacques Derrida, who construes the consequences of the philosophy-language relation, of our finitude in relation to both, in ways that bear directly upon how we may and may not think our relations to ourselves and to nonhuman animals.

Diamond's earlier work is worth revisiting here in some detail because it addresses even more methodically the relations among language, thinking, and our ethical obligations to nonhuman others that form the focus of this volume. As she insists in an essay from 2001 called "Injustice and Animals," our "grammatical redescription" of a philosophical problem is crucial and in some sense determinative of our ability to do justice to the ethical challenges it entails.[7] In this light, for her, the fundamental question of *justice* issues from an essentially different conceptual realm than the question of "rights." "When genuine issues of justice and injustice are framed in terms of rights," she argues, "they are thereby distorted and trivialized" because of "the underlying tie between rights and a system of entitlement that is concerned, not with evil done to a person, but with how much he or she gets compared to other participants in the system" (121). In rights discourse, she argues, "the *character* of our conflicts is made obscure" by what Wittgenstein would call a poor grammatical description of the problem of justice (124).

Instead, what generates our moral response to animals and their treatment, Diamond argues, is our sense of the mortality and vulnerability that we share with them, of which the brute subjection of the body—in the treatment of animals as mere research tools, say—is perhaps the most poignant testament. For Diamond, the "horror at the conceptualizing of animals as putting nothing in the way of their use as mere stuff" is dependent upon "a comparable horror at human relentlessness and pitiliness in the exercise of power" toward other humans (as, in for example, the torture of other human beings) ("Injustice," 136). What the rights tradition misses, in her view, is that the "capacity to respond to injustice as injustice" depends not on working out (from a safe ontological distance, as it were) who should have a fair share of this or that abstract "good," based upon the possession of this or that abstract "interest" or attribute, but rather on "a recognition of *our own* vulnerability"—a recognition not demanded and in some sense actively avoided by rights-oriented thinking ("Injustice," 121). (And here, of course, we would do well to remember the "wounded" character of Coetzee's

Elizabeth Costello, a rawness that pushes her moral response to our treatment of animals beyond propositional argument—and sometimes beyond the decorum of polite society.)

What such an insight points toward, Diamond contends, is the fact that "there is something wrong with the contrast, taken to be exhaustive, between demanding one's rights and begging for kindness—begging for what is *merely* kindness. The idea that *those* are the only possibilities is . . . one of the main props of the idea that doing injustice *is* failing to respect rights" ("Injustice," 129). Contemporary moral theory thus "pushes apart justice, on the one hand, and compassion, love, pity, tenderness, on the other" (131), but Diamond's understanding of the question "has at its center the idea that a kind of loving attention to another being, a possible victim of injustice, is essential to any understanding of the evil of injustice" (131–32). In fact, she agrees with Simone Weil's suggestion that "rights can work for justice or for injustice," that the concept of rights possesses "a kind of moral noncommitment to the good" (128). In an important sense, then, "rights" are beside the point of justice per se, and "the language of rights is, one might say, meant to be useful in contexts in which we cannot count on the kind of understanding of evil that depends on loving attention to the victim" (139).

There are, in other words, two different and in fact incommensurable kinds of value here (121)—a point missed by *both* "sides" of what Diamond calls "that great arena of dissociated thought, contemporary debate about animals' rights."[8] The problem with *both* sides of the debate—represented by, say, Peter Singer, on one side, and, on the other, philosopher Michael Leahy and his avatar Thomas O'Hearne in *The Lives of Animals*—is that they are locked into a model of justice in which a being does or does not have rights on the basis of its possession (or lack) of morally significant characteristics that can be empirically derived. Both sides argue "that what is involved in moral thought is knowledge of empirical similarities and differences, and the testing and application of general principles of evaluation."[9] And so, as Diamond puts it in the essay included here, "the opposite sides in the debate may have more in common then they realize. In the voices we hear in the debate about animal rights, those of people like Singer on the one hand and those of Leahy and the fictional O'Hearne on the other, there is shared a desire for a 'because': because animals are this kind of being, or because they are that kind of being, thus-and-such is their standing for our moral thought" ("The Difficulty of Reality," 71). But what Diamond hears in *both* sets of voices is an evasion of our "exposure" to an arena of moral complexity in which (to quote Cavell) "the other can present me with no mark or feature on the basis of which I can *settle* my attitude" (quoted in "The Difficulty of Reality," 71–72).

Part of the reason for that, of course, is that such attitudes are far from the thin, if-P-then-Q abstractions that a certain kind of philosophy takes them to be. They are thick with psychological vexation and rife with contradictory impulses and attachments. So Diamond is concerned to show not just that such a picture of ethics confuses the question of justice with the "mediocre" level of mere rights ("Injustice and Animals," 121) but also that it bears no resemblance to what she suggests is our moral *life*. For her, proponents of animal rights in the analytical tradition are wrong when they insist that the distinction between human and animal is not ethically fundamental. At the same time, however, those who *oppose* animal rights within that same analytical tradition are wrong about how the difference between humans and animals *is* relevant. "The notion 'human being' is of the greatest significance in moral thought" ("Losing Your Concepts," 264), she argues, but not because it is a "biological notion" (264). Rather, the concept of "human being" is a main source of that moral sensibility that we may *then* be able to extend to nonhuman animals. "We can come to think of killing an animal as in some circumstances at least similar to homicide," she continues, "but the significance of doing so depends on our already having an idea of what it is to kill a man; and for us (as opposed to abstract Moral Agents) the idea of what it is to kill a man does depend on the sense of human life as special, as some-

thing set apart from what else happens on the planet"
("Experimenting," 353).

For Diamond, then, it is crucial to take account of
"what human beings have *made of* the difference between human beings and animals" ("Experimenting,"
351). As she puts it elsewhere,

> if we appeal to people to prevent suffering, and we, in
> our appeal, try to obliterate the distinction between
> human beings and animals and just get people to
> speak or think of "different species of animals,"
> there is no footing left from which to tell us what we
> ought to do. . . . The moral expectations of other hu-
> man beings demand something of me as other than
> an animal; and we do something like imaginatively
> read into animals something like such expectations
> when we think of vegetarianism as enabling us to
> meet a cow's eyes. There is nothing wrong with that;
> there *is* something wrong with trying to keep that
> response and destroy its foundation.[10]

So for Diamond, it is not by denying the special status of "human being" but rather, as it were, by intensifying it that we can come to think of nonhuman animals
not as bearers of "interests" or as "rights holders" but
rather as something much more compelling: "fellow
creatures." That phrase "does not mean, biologically,
an animal, something with *biological* life," but rather

our "response to animals as our fellows in mortality, in life on this earth" ("Eating," 329). And hence, the difference between human and nonhuman animals "may indeed start out as a biological difference, but it becomes something for human thought through being taken up and made something *of*—by generations of human beings, in their practices, their art, their literature, their religion" ("Experimenting," 351), those practices that enable us to "imaginatively read into animals" expectations that originate, as it were, in the human, the "other than an animal."

At this juncture, Diamond's work is worth comparing, I think, with Jacques Derrida's recent investigations of what he calls "the question of the animal." At first glance, Derrida's work seems remarkably consonant with Diamond's, beginning with three main features. First, Derrida emphasizes, like Diamond, the fundamental ethical bond we have with nonhuman animals as residing in our shared finitude, our vulnerability and mortality as "fellow creatures" (a phrase he, too, invokes at key moments in his argument). Second, Derrida shares with Diamond a certain understanding of what ethics is: not propositionally deriving a set of rules for conduct that apply generically in all cases but rather confronting our "exposure" to a permanent condition in which (to use Cavell's phrase) "there is no way to settle our attitude." And third, Derrida also insists that crucial to both of these is "to show," as Diamond puts it in an earlier essay, "how philosophical misconceptions about language are connected with blindness to what our conceptual life is like" ("Losing Your Concepts," 263).

As for the first point, Derrida in his late work turns, oddly enough, to the philosopher who is central to Peter Singer's work, the utilitarian Jeremy Bentham. But what Derrida draws from Bentham's famous contention that the fundamental ethical question with animals is not "can they talk?" or "can they reason?" but "can they *suffer*?" is something quite different from (and finally opposed to) Singer's derivation of animals' fundamental "interests." For Derrida, putting the question in this way "changes everything" because philosophy from Aristotle to Levinas has posed the question of the animal in terms of capacities (prototypically, for reason or language), which in turn "determines so many others concerning *power* or *capability* [*pouvoirs*], and *attributes* [*avoirs*]: being able, having the power to give, to die, to bury one's dead, to dress, to work, to invent a technique."[11] What makes Bentham's reframing of the problem so powerful for Derrida is that now "the question is disturbed by a certain *passivity*. It bears witness, manifesting already, as question, the response that testifies to sufferance, a passion, a not-being-able." "What of the vulnerability felt on the basis of this inability?" he continues; "what is this non-power at the heart of power? . . . What right should be accorded it? To what extent does it concern us?" It concerns us very directly, of course, because "mortality resides there, as the most radical means of thinking the finitude that we share with animals, the mortality that belongs to the very finitude of life, to the experience of compassion . . . the anguish of this vulnerability" ("The Animal," 396).

In Derrida as in Diamond, then, the vulnerability and finitude that we share with nonhuman animals and the compassion that this commonality makes possible are at the very core of the question of ethics—not just "mere" kindness, but *justice*. As Derrida puts it, "what is still presented in such a problematic way as *animal rights*" has a force quite independent of—and if we believe Diamond, quite antithetical to[12]—the philosophical framework that usually accompanies it. For Derrida, as well, the point of the animal rights movement, however flawed its articulation, is "to awaken us to our responsibilities and our obligations with respect to the living in general, and precisely to this fundamental compassion that, were we to take it seriously, would have to change even the very basis . . . of the philosophical problematic of the animal" ("The Animal," 395). And it is this very shifting of the terms of the problematic that Diamond finds Coetzee cagily using the difference between literature and "philosophy" to stage—a fact not quite grasped in her view by the philosophical commentaries appended to the end of *The Lives of Animals*.

This leads, in turn, to the second important point of contact between Diamond's work and Derrida's. For both, the question of the animal requires an alternative conception of ethics to what we find in the liberal justice and rights tradition of analytical philosophy as it manifests itself in work such as Singer's. For Singer, as we have seen, ethics means the application of what Derrida will elsewhere characterize as a "calculable process"[13]—in Singer's case, it is quite literally the utilitarian calculus that would tally up the "interests" of the particular beings in question in a given situation, regardless of their species, and would determine what counts as a just act by calculating which action maximizes the greatest good for the greatest number. In doing so, however, Singer would reduce ethics to the very antithesis of ethics in Diamond's and Derrida's terms because he would overleap what Derrida calls "the ordeal of the undecidable," which "must be gone through by any decision worthy of the name" ("Force," 24). For Derrida, "A decision that didn't go through the ordeal of the undecidable would not be a free decision, it would only be the programmable application or unfolding of a calculable process. It might be legal; it would not be just" ("Force," 24). "Ordeal" is indeed the word we want here, which is one reason Diamond rivets our attention more than once on Elizabeth Coetzee's "rawness" of nerves, her sufferance of a responsibility that is both undeniable and unappeasable. But what the rights view of ethics gives us instead is a "de-flection" of this fully ethical ordeal, one in which, as Diamond puts it, "we would be *given* the presence or absence of moral community (or thus-and-such degree or kind of moral community) with animals" ("The Dif-ficulty of Reality," 72).

Aside from being the very antithesis of the ethical in Diamond's and Derrida's sense, such a "calculation," in its empirical derivation of the shared "interests" of human and nonhuman animals—what Diamond calls our "properties," our "marks and features" ("The Dif-ficulty of Reality," 72)—confuses what Diamond calls "biological concepts" with the concepts proper to *ethi-cal* thought. This is what Derrida has in mind (and more, as we are about to see) in his criticism of a "bio-logical continuism, whose sinister connotations we are well aware of," one that ignores "the abyssal rupture" between human and nonhuman forms of life.[14] He has "thus never believed," he writes, "in some homo-geneous continuity between what calls *itself* man and what *he* calls the animal" ("The Animal," 398).

At this juncture, however—and it is marked quite precisely by Derrida's emphasis on "what calls *itself* man and what *he* calls the animal"—some fundamen-tal differences between Derrida and Diamond begin to come into view, not least of all in the articulation of this peculiar thing called "the human." We can be-gin to get a sense of this difference by returning to the crucial role that vulnerability, passivity, and mortality play here for both Diamond and Derrida. Let us recall Diamond's contention that "we can come to think of killing an animal as in some circumstances at least similar to homicide, but the significance of doing so depends on our already having an idea of what it is to kill a man" ("Experimenting," 353). Such an idea depends, however, on a relation to our *own* mortality that is rejected in Derrida's work. For Derrida, contra Diamond, we *never* have an idea of what death is *for us*—indeed, death is precisely that which can never be *for us*—and if we did, then the ethical relation to the other would be immediately foreclosed.

This is clearest, perhaps, in Derrida's reading of Heidegger and his concept of "being-toward-death," a concept that appears—but only appears—to do justice to the passivity and finitude in which the ethical resides. As Richard Bearsdsworth characterizes it, from Derrida's point of view, Heidegger *appropriates* the limit of death "rather than returning it to *the other* of time. In Beardsworth's words, "The existential of 'being-towards-death' is consequently a 'being-able' (*pouvoir-etre*), not the impossibility of all power" whose radical passivity and vulnerability ties the self to the other in an ethical relation. As he explains, for Derrida,

the "impossibility" of death for the ego confirms that the experience of finitude is one of radical passivity. That the "I" cannot experience its "own" death means, firstly, that death is an immanence *without* horizon, and secondly, that time is that which exceeds my death, that time is the generation which precedes and follows me. . . . Death is not a limit or horizon which, re-cognized, allows the ego to assume the "there" [as in Heidegger's "being-to-ward-death"]; it is something that never arrives in the ego's time, a "not-yet" which confirms the priority of time over the ego, marking, accordingly, the precedence of the other over the ego.[15]

For Derrida, then, "no relation to death can appear as such," and "if there is no 'as' to death," then the "relation to death is always mediated through an other. The 'as' of death always appears *through* an other's death, *for* another" (Beardsworth, *Derrida*, 118). In Derrida's words: "The death of the other thus becomes . . . 'first,' always first" (quoted in Beardsworth, *Derrida*, 119). Hence, Beardsworth argues, "The recognition of the limit of death is always through another and is, therefore, at the same time the recognition of the other" (118). And since the same is true *of* the other in relation to its *own* death, what this means is that "death *im*possibilizes existence" and does so both for me *and* for the other—since death can no more *be* "for" the other than it can for me (132). But it is, paradoxically, in just this impossibility that the possibility of justice resides, the (as it were) permanent call of the other in the face of which the subject always arrives "too late." Or, to put this is somewhat different terms, when Diamond affirms Costello's assertion that "I know what it is like to be a corpse," Derrida's response would be, "No, you don't. Only the other does, and for that you are held hostage (to use Levinas's term) in unappeasable ethical debt to the other"—hence the otherwise odd idea of the "gift" of death (to borrow from Derrida's book by the same title). To put it another way, there is the suggestion in Diamond, I think, that imaginative and literary projection can somehow achieve in this instance what propositional, syllogistic philosophy cannot achieve (the nonconceptual, nonlogical force of "I know what it's like to be a corpse"), but Derrida would see this, too, as a "deflection" of "exposure": exposure not just to mortality but also to a certain estranging operation of language, to a *second* kind of finitude whose implications are enormous (a point I'll return to in a moment).

Such is the full resonance, I think, of Derrida's contention with regard to Bentham that "the word *can* [*pouvoir*] changes sense and sign here once one asks 'can they suffer?' The word wavers henceforth. As soon as such a question is posed what counts is not only the idea of a transitivity or activity (being able to speak, to reason, and so on); *the important thing is rather what impels it towards self-contradiction, something we will later relate back to auto-biography*" ("The

Animal," 396; emphasis mine). What Derrida has in mind by the "auto-" of "auto-biography" is exemplified, I think, in Diamond's picture of the human in relation to ethics, a picture in which, as in Heidegger, vulnerability, passivity, and finitude appear to be recuperated as a "being-able" and a "transitivity" that, despite itself, reontologizes the split between the human and the animal, across which the human then reaches, as it were, in an act of benevolence toward an other that we "imagine" is enough like us to warrant ethical treatment. This seems clear enough, for example, in Diamond's contention, which I mentioned earlier, that "the moral expectations of other human beings demand something of me as other than an animal; and we do something like imaginatively read into animals something like such expectations when we think of vegetarianism as enabling us to meet a cow's eyes" ("Eating," 333). And it is also underscored by her contention in the same essay that "our *hearing* the moral appeal of an animal is our hearing it speak—as it were—the language of our fellow human beings" ("Eating," 333–34).

Part of the strength and attraction of Diamond's remarkable essay "The Difficulty of Reality and the Difficulty of Philosophy," I think, is that it in a sense moves beyond—or perhaps I should say, moves *without*—this sort of formulation of the relations among ethics, language, and species difference. In this sense, the essay's strength is precisely its weakness. Where the emphasis in earlier essays was on our *ability* (Derrida's *pouvoirs*) to *extend* imaginatively an apparently secure sense of "the human" to animals (hearing them "speak our language," seeing in them expectations of us as "other than animal"), here, when we try to put into words the experience of "the difficulty of reality" that we find bodied forth in Ted Hughes's "Six Young Men" or Coetzee's *The Lives of Animals*, "the words fail us, the words don't do what we are trying to get them to do. The words make it look as if I am simply unable to see over a wall which happens to separate me from something I very much want to see. But the fact that the words are apparently too weak to do what I am demanding from them does not mean that the experience here of *powerlessness* has been shown to involve a kind of grammatical error" (67).

The force of this turn in Diamond's thought and its consequences for ethics can be extended and elaborated, I think, by means of Derrida's work, which would help us to articulate more fully the implications of the fact that there are *two* kinds of finitude here, *two* kinds of passivity and vulnerability, and that the first type (physical vulnerability, embodiment, and eventually mortality) is paradoxically made unavailable, *inappropriable* to us by the very thing that makes it available—namely, a second type of "passivity" or "not being able," which is the finitude we experience in our subjection to a radically ahuman technicity or mechanicity of language, a technicity which has profound consequences, of course, for what we too hastily think of as "our" concepts, which are therefore in an important sense not "ours" at all.

And here, then, we arrive at the third point of contact—but also finally of difference—between Diamond and Derrida that I noted above: "how philosophical misconceptions about language are connected with blindness to what our conceptual life is like," to use Diamond's phrase. For Derrida's point would be not only that "we" *don't* have a concept of "the human" but also that it's a good thing, too, because it is only on the strength of that weakness, you might say, that we are able to avoid both horns of the dilemma brought to light in Diamond's work: on the one hand, the constant threat of ethnocentrism that a certain understanding of Wittgenstein flirts with (we do what we do because of "what we have made of the difference between humans and animals," which keeps us from lapsing into "biological continuism"); and, on the other hand, the mining for ethical "universals" that, for philosophers such as Singer and Regan, would attempt to counter this very threat by uncovering first principles of ethics via the anti-ethnocentric autonomy of "reason." Derrida, I am suggesting, makes available a "third way," whose response would be that, yes, it is true that what we think of as the "principles" of personhood, morality, and so on are inseparable from who "we" are, from our discourse as a "mode of life" (to put it in Wittgenstein's terms). But, at the same time, "we" are not "we"; we are not that "auto-" of "autobiography" (as in Derrida's "The Autobiographical Animal") that humanism "gives to itself." Rather, "we" are always radically other, already in- or ahuman in our very being—not just in the evolutionary, biological, and zoological fact of our physical vulnerability and mortality, our mammalian existence, of course, but also in our subjection to and constitution in the materiality and technicity of a language that is always on the scene before we are, as a precondition of our subjectivity. And this means that "what *he* calls 'man,'" what "we" call "we," always covers over a more radical "not being able" that makes our very conceptual life possible. Even more important, perhaps—at least for the topic at hand—is that this passivity and subjection are shared by humans and nonhumans the moment they begin to interact and communicate by means of any semiotic system. As Derrida puts it in a well-known passage from the interview " 'Eating Well' ":

> If one reinscribes language in a network of possibilities that do not merely encompass it but mark it irreducibly from the inside, everything changes. I am thinking in particular of the mark in general, of the trace, of iterability, of *différance*. These possibilities

or necessities, without which there would be no language, *are themselves not only human. . . .* And what I am proposing here should allow us to take into account scientific knowledge about the complexity of "animal languages," genetic coding, all forms of marking within which so-called human language, as original as it might be, does not allow us to 'cut' once and for all where we would in general like to cut.[16]

There is no need to rehearse here Derrida's theorization of iterabilty, *différance*, trace, and so on; rather, I simply want to mark how this second kind of "not being able" renders uncertain and unstable—"unsettled," in Cavell's terms—the relationship of the human to itself because it renders unstable not just the boundary between human and animal but also that between the organic and the mechanical or technological. And for these very reasons—because of the estrangement of the "the human" from the "auto-" that "we" give to ourselves—the relation between the human and nonhuman animals is constantly opened anew and, as it were, permanently. It is a "wound," if you will, that can never be healed. Derrrida summarizes this in a 2004 interview:

Beginning with *Of Grammatology*, the elaboration of a new concept of the *trace* had to be extended to the entire field of the living, *or rather to the life/death relation*, beyond the anthropological limits of "spoken" language. . . . At the time I stressed that the "concepts of writing, trace, gramma, or grapheme" exceeded the opposition "human/nonhuman." All the deconstructive gestures I have attempted to perform on philosophical texts . . . consist in questioning the self-interested misrecognition of what is called the Animal in general, and the way in which these interpret the border between Man and Animal.[17]

I stress this intercalation of the boundary between the biological/organic and the mechanical/technical in relation to the infra- and transhuman in no small part because Diamond herself is very interested in it—most conspicuously, of course, in her reading of the "exposure" of the photograph in Ted Hughes's "Six Young Men"—a technological, archival artifact that confronts us with "a shuddering awareness of death and life together" ("The Difficulty of Reality," 73). Here, however, Diamond and Derrida pull us in different and perhaps even opposite directions, for Diamond then glosses that "exposure" in terms of Elizabeth Costello's contention, "I know what it is like to be a corpse"—a contention whose significance she unpacks along the following lines in the final paragraph of her essay, as a kind of rejoinder to pragmatism: "A language, a form of thought, cannot (we may be told) get things right or wrong, fit or fail to fit reality; it can only be more or less useful. What

I want to end with is not exactly a response to that: it is to note how much that coming apart of thought and reality belongs to flesh and blood" (78). Derrida's point, however, is that this "coming apart" is not *just* of flesh and blood but is also born of the fact that our *relation* to flesh and blood is fatefully constituted by a technicity with which it is prosthetically entwined, a diacritical, semiotic machine of language in the broadest sense that exceeds any and all presence, including our own.[18]

That it *is* "in the broadest sense" can be brought out, I think, by looking briefly at Derrida's own confrontation with an "exposure" of the sort Diamond is interested in—in this case, an exposure of a piece of film. In a set of conversations with Bernard Stiegler published in English under the title *Echographies of Television*, Derrida is concerned to differ with Roland Barthes's suggestion in *Camera Lucida* that "the photo is literally an emanation of the referent. From a real body which was there proceed radiations that come to touch me, I who am here. . . . A kind of umbilical cord ties the body of the photographic thing to my gaze."[19] Instead, Derrida insists that "the modern possibility of the photograph joins, in a single system, death and the referent" (*Echographies*, 115). What he means by this rather enigmatic formulation is that a kind of "spectrality" inheres in the technology of the image because of its fundamental iterability:

As soon as there is a technology of the image, visibility brings night. . . . [B]ecause we know that, once it has been taken, captured, this image will be reproducible in our absence, because we know this *already*, we are already haunted by this future, which brings our death. Our disappearance is already here. . . . And this is what makes our experience so strange. We are spectralized by the shot, captured or possessed by spectrality in advance.

What has, dare I say, constantly haunted me in this logic of the specter is that it regularly exceeds all the oppositions between visible and invisible, sensible and insensible. A specter is both visible and invisible, both phenomenal and nonphenomenal: a trace that marks the present with its absence in advance. (117)

Derrida then tells a story that is haunting in its own right about his participation in the Ken McMullen film *Ghostdance*, where he improvised a scene with French actress Pascale Ogier, in which he asks her, "And what about you, do you believe in ghosts?" and she replies "Yes, now I do, yes." "But imagine the experience I had," Derrida says,

when, two or three years later, after Pascale Ogier had died, I watched the film again in the United States, at the request of students who wanted to discuss it with me. Suddenly I saw Pascal's face, which I knew was a dead woman's face, come onto the screen. She answered my questions: "Do you believe in ghosts?" Practically looking me in the eye, she said to me again, on the big screen: "Yes, now I do, yes." Which now? . . . I had the unnerving sense of the return of her specter, the specter of her specter coming back to say to me—to me here, now: "Now . . . now . . . now, that is to say, in this dark room on another continent, in another world, here, now, yes, believe me, I believe in ghosts."

But at the same time, I know that the first time Pascale said this, already, when she repeated this in my office, already, this spectrality was at work. It was already there, she was already saying this, and she knew, just as we know, that even if she hadn't died in the interval, one day, it would be a dead woman who said, "I am dead," or "I am dead, I know what I'm talking about from where I am, and I'm watching you," and this gaze remained dissymmetrical, exchanged beyond all possible exchange . . . the other gaze met, in an infinite night.   (120)

So here is Elizabeth Costello again, then, in a different light: "What I know is what a corpse cannot know: that it is extinct, that it knows nothing and will never know anything anymore. For an instant, before my whole structure of knowledge collapses in panic, I am alive inside that contradiction, dead and alive at the same time" (quoted in Diamond, "The Difficulty of Reality," 74). And here is Hughes, by the light of day that is also the light of death, the light of night:

> That man's not more alive whom you confront
> And shake by the hand, see hale, hear speak loud,
> Than any of these six celluloid smiles are,
> Nor prehistoric or fabulous beast more dead;
> No thought so vivid as their smoking blood:
> To regard this photograph might well dement,
> Such contradictory permanent horrors here
> Smile from the single exposure and shoulder out
> One's own body from its instant and heat.

In the end, however—and this is the final difference between the Cavell/Diamond line and Derrida that I will want to mark—Derrida derives from this "dementing" force, which bleeds together organism and machine, living and dead, "prehistoric beast" and one's own human "instant and heat," a kind of law or general economy, the fundaments of which reach all the way back to his earliest work. As he puts it in *Echographies of Television* (and this descends directly from my earlier discussion of the non-appropriability of death that constitutes my indebtedness to the other), this relationship constitutes an "inheritance," a "genealogy of the law" (122); before the specter of the dead we are " 'before the law,' without any possible symmetry, without reciprocity" (120):

The wholly other—and the dead person is the wholly other—watches me, concerns me, and concerns or watches me while addressing to me, without however answering me, a prayer or an injunction, an infinite demand, which becomes the law for me: it concerns me, it regards me, it addresses itself only to me at the same time that it exceeds me infinitely and universally, without my being able to exchange a glance with him or with her. (120–21)

This is most obvious, perhaps, in the most well-known example of the spectral phenomenon that Derrida discusses—Shakespeare's *Hamlet*, where the relationship between inheritance, law, responsibility, and spectrality is particularly (even Oedipally) pronounced—but it would also seem to be the case with Hughes's six young men in the photograph, to whom we, as the living, feel a strange kind of responsibility and debt that is unsettling because unanswerable, a point powerfully put in motion early in Diamond's essay. In Derrida's words: "the other comes *before* me" (122).

In Derrida's derivation of a general economy or "law" of "heteronomy" from this spectrality, Diamond and Cavell would no doubt find him seeking his own kind of solace, engaging in his own kind of "deflection" by the force of reason that they see their philosophy as dedicated to resisting. For what is lost in such a foreclosure, in their view, is the rawness testified to by an

Elizabeth Costello and the ethical stakes of attending to that rawness, of not making it (as Diamond might put it) just another example of some general principle. As Cavell has put it elsewhere in his discussion of Derrida's critique of J. L. Austin's "phonocentrism," the problem with the Derridean strategy is that its emphasis on the general economy of iterability is a kind of "deflecting attention, as rushing too quickly away from, the act or encounter entailed in the historical and individual process of inheriting" (*Quest*, 131) a process that involves not the overcoming of the voice but its assumption or "arrogation," as Cavell puts it.[20] For Cavell, the problem with the Derridean general economy—and the critique of phonocentrism is only one example of it—is that it continues the project of metaphysics while announcing metaphysics' demise, and it does so in flight from the "ordinary," the "everyday," and its power to "shoulder us out from our light and heat." "The metaphysician in each of us," Cavell writes, "will use metaphysics to get out of the moral of the ordinary, out of our ordinary moral obligations" (*Passages*, 74–75), out of "the responsibility you bear—or take, or find, or disclaim—for your words" (*Quest*, 135), because metaphysics "names our wish (and the possibility of our wishing) to strip ourselves of the responsibility we have in meaning." "Such courses," Cavell suggests, "seem to give up the game; they do not achieve what freedom, what useful ideal of myself, there may be for me, but seem as self-imposed as the grandest philosophy—or, as Heidegger might almost have put it, as unself-imposed" (*Quest*, 131).

Given the date of its rendering (1988), Cavell's observation could not have taken account of Derrida's later work on the animal, in particular "The Animal That Therefore I Am (More to Follow)" (2002), which presents less a token for a systematic philosophy than a limit before which we are in a profound sense interrogated and humbled. As Derrida writes of being stared at by his cat (in a moment either famous or notorious, depending on your point of view), he finds himself literally naked and, in Diamond's terms, exposed:

> No, no, my cat, the cat that looks at me in my bedroom or in the bathroom, this cat . . . does not appear here as representative, or ambassador, carrying the immense symbolic responsibility. . . . If I say "it is a real cat" that sees me naked, it is in order to mark its unsubstitutable singularity. . . . I see it as *this* irreplaceable living being that one day enters my space, enters this place where it can encounter me, see me, even see me naked. Nothing can ever take away from me the certainty that what we have here is an existence that refuses to be conceptualized
> ("The Animal," 378–79)

And so, he suggests, "the gaze called animal"—and that qualification, "*called* animal," is important—

offers to my sight the abyssal limit of the human: the inhuman or the ahuman, the ends of man, that is to say the bordercrossing from which vantage man dares to announce himself to himself, thereby calling himself by the name that he believes he gives himself. And in these moments of nakedness, under the gaze of the animal, everything can happen to me, I am like a child ready for the apocalypse. *I am (following) the apocalypse itself,* that is to say the ultimate and first event of the end, the unveiling and the verdict. ("The Animal," 381–82)

If such is the case, then we are led back, perhaps, to where we began, in all its vexation and rawness: to David Lurie parked on the side of the road, weeping, wondering what has overtaken him; and to Elizabeth Costello, who, in confessing to her son just how haunted she is by the specter of our fellow creatures and the infernal holocaust we have inflicted on them, presses upon herself the question to which this volume offers not an answer, exactly, but a kind of understanding: "I no longer know where I am. . . . Yet I'm not dreaming. I look into your eyes . . . and I see only kindness, human-kindness. Calm down, I tell myself, you are making a mountain out of a molehill. This is life. Everyone else comes to terms with it, why can't you? *Why can't you?*" (69).

NOTES

1. J. M. Coetzee, *Disgrace* (New York: Penguin, 1999), 43. Further references are given in the text.

2. J. M. Coetzee, *The Lives of Animals*, ed. and intro. Amy Gutmann (Princeton, N.J.: Princeton University Press, 1999), 43. Further references are in the text.

3. Stanley Cavell, *In Quest of the Ordinary: Lines of Skepticism and Romanticism* (Chicago: University of Chicago Press, 1988), 31. Further references are in the text.

4. Stanley Cavell, *This New Yet Unapproachable America* (Albuquerque, N.M.: Living Batch Press, 1989), 86. Further references are given in the text.

5. Stanley Cavell, *Conditions Handsome and Unhandsome: The Constitution of Emersonian Perfectionism* (Chicago: University of Chicago Press, 1990), 38–39. Further references are in the text. I have discussed the similarities—but also the important differences—between Cavell and Derrida around Heidegger's figure of the hand in "In the Shadow of Wittgenstein's Lion," in *Zoontologies: The Question of the Animal*, ed. Cary Wolfe (Minneapolis: University of Minnesota Press, 2003), 20–21.

6. Jacques Derrida, "*Geschlecht* II: Heidegger's Hand," trans. John P. Leavey Jr., in *Deconstruction and Philosophy*, ed. John Sallis (Chicago: University of Chicago Press, 1986), 173. Further references are in the text.

7. Cora Diamond, "Injustice and Animals," in *Slow Cures and Bad Philosophers: Essays on Wittgenstein, Medi-*

cine, and Bioethics, ed. Carl Elliott (Durham, N.C.: Duke University Press, 2001), 123. Further references are given in the text.

8. Cora Diamond, "Losing Your Concepts," *Ethics* 98, no. 2 (January 1998): 276. Further references are in the text.

9. Cora Diamond, "Experimenting on Animals: A Problem in Ethics," in *The Realistic Spirit: Wittgenstein, Philosophy, and the Mind* (Cambridge, Mass.: MIT Press, 1991), 350. Further references are given in the text.

10. Cora Diamond, "Eating Meat and Eating People," in *The Realistic Spirit: Wittgenstein, Philosophy, and the Mind* (Cambridge: Mass.: MIT Press, 1991), 333. Further references are given in the text.

11. Jacques Derrida, "The Animal That Therefore I Am (More to Follow)," trans. David Wills, *Critical Inquiry* 28 (Winter 2002): 386, 395. Further references are given in the text.

12. For Diamond's explicit discussion of animal rights and the difference between animal rights and animal welfare, see "Injustice and Animals," 141–42.

13. Jacques Derrida, "Force of Law: The 'Mystical Foundation of Authority,'" trans. Mary Quaintance, in *Deconstruction and the Possibility of Justice*, ed. Drucila Cornell, Michal Rosenfeld, and David Gray Carlson (London: Routledge, 1992), 24. Further references are given in the text.

14. As Derrida has suggested in his reading of Heidegger and the animal in *Of Spirit: Heidegger and the Question*, trans. Geoffrey Bennington and Rachel Bowlby

(Chicago: University of Chicago Press, 1989), those "sinister connotations" of "continuism"—which Heidegger's humanist separation of human and animal is dead-set against—include racism, the use of naturalism to countenance xenophobia, and much else besides (56).

15. Richard Beardsworth, *Derrida and the Political* (London: Routledge, 1996), 130–31. Further references are given in the text.

16. Jacques Derrida, "'Eating Well,' or The Calculation of the Subject: An Interview with Jacques Derrida," in *Who Comes After the Subject?*, ed. Eduardo Cadava, Peter Connor, and Jean-Luc Nancy (New York: Routledge, 1991), 116–17.

17. Jacques Derrida, "Violence Against Animals," in Jacques Derrida and Elisabeth Roudinesco, *For What Tomorrow . . . : A Dialgoue*, trans. Jeff Fort (Stanford, Calif.: Stanford University Press, 2004), 63; emphasis mine.

18. For a brilliant exploration of the technicity and mechanicity of language in relation to prosthetics and the question of technology, see David Wills, *Thinking Back: Dorsality, Technology, Politics* (Minneapolis: University of Minnesota Press, forthcoming), and his earlier volume *Prosthesis* (Stanford, Calif.: Stanford University Press, 1995).

19. Roland Barthes, *Camera Lucida: Reflections on Photography*, trans. Richard Howard (New York: Hill and Wang, 1981), 76, 80–81; quoted in Jacques Derrida and Bernard Stiegler, *Echographies of Television*, trans. Jennifer Bajorek (Cambridge: Polity Press, 2002), 113. Further references are given in the text.

20. On the "arrogation" of voice, see chapter 1 of Stanley Cavell, *A Pitch of Philosophy* (Cambridge, Mass.: Harvard University Press, 1995). His engagement with Derrida's reading of Austin takes place both in Stanley Cavell, *Philosophical Passages: Wittgenstein, Emerson, Austin, Derrida* (Oxford: Basil Blackwell, 1995), 42–90, and in the chapter "Counter-Philosophy and the Pawn of Voice," in *A Pitch of Philosophy*, 53–128. Further references to both books are in the text.

ONE

THE DIFFICULTY OF REALITY AND THE DIFFICULTY OF PHILOSOPHY

CORA DIAMOND

I am concerned in this paper with a range of phenomena, which, in the first four sections of the paper, I shall suggest by some examples. In the last three sections, I try to connect the topic thus indicated with the thought of Stanley Cavell.

I. A SINGLE EXPOSURE

First example: a poem of Ted Hughes's, from the mid-50s, called "Six Young Men". The speaker in the poem looks at a photo of six smiling young men, seated in a familiar spot. He knows the bank covered with bilberries, the tree and the old wall in the photo; the six men in the picture would have heard the valley below them

43

sounding with rushing water, just as it still does. Four decades have faded the photo; it came from 1914. The men are profoundly, fully alive, one bashfully lowering his eyes, one chewing a piece of grass, one "is ridiculous with cocky pride". Within six months of the picture's having been taken, all six were dead. In the photograph, then, there can also be thought the death of these men: the worst "flash and rending" of war falling onto these smiles now forty years rotted and gone.

Here is the last stanza:

That man's not more alive whom you confront
And shake by the hand, see hale, hear speak loud,
Than any of these six celluloid smiles are,
Nor prehistoric or fabulous beast more dead;
No thought so vivid as their smoking blood:
To regard this photograph might well dement,
Such contradictory permanent horrors here
Smile from the single exposure and shoulder out
One's own body from its instant and heat.

What interests me there is the experience of the mind's not being able to encompass something which it encounters. It is capable of making one go mad to try, to bring together in thought what cannot be thought: the impossibility of anyone's being more alive than these smiling men, nothing's being more dead. (No one is more alive than is the person looking at the photo; no one is more alive than you are, reading the poem. In Part VI, I turn back to the 'contradictory permanent horrors' of the imagination of death.)

Now it's plainly possible to describe the photo so it does not seem boggling at all. It is a photo of men who died young, not long after the picture was taken. Where is the contradiction?—Taking the picture that way, there is no problem about our concepts being adequate to describe it. Again, one might think of how one would teach a child who had been shown a photo and told it was a photo of her grandfather, whom she knows to be dead. If she asks, "Why is he smiling if he's dead?", she might be told that he was smiling when the picture was taken, because he was not dead then, and that he died later. The child is being taught the language-game, being shown how her problem disappears as she comes to see how things are spoken of in the game. The point of view from which she sees a problem is not yet in the game; while that from which the horrible contradiction impresses itself on the poet-speaker is that of someone who can no longer speak within the game. Language is shouldered out from the game, as the body from its instant and heat.

What Hughes gives us is a case of what I want to call the difficulty of reality. That is a phrase of John Updike's,[1] which I want to pick up for the phenomena with which I am concerned, experiences in which we take something in reality to be resistant to our thinking it, or possibly to be painful in its inexplicability, difficult in that way, or perhaps awesome and astonishing in its inexplicability. *We take things so.* And the things we take so may simply not, to others, present the kind of difficulty, of being hard or impossible or agonizing to get one's mind round.

II. A WOUNDED ANIMAL

> Few of us are not in some way infirm, or even diseased; and our very infirmities help us unexpectedly.
> —William James, *The Varieties of Religious Experience*

Second example. The example is complex: part of it is the set of lectures delivered by the South African novelist J. M. Coetzee as his Tanner Lectures. These lectures were published under the title *The Lives of Animals*, together with an introduction by Amy Gutmann and comments by several other people; the introduction and comments also form part of the example as I want to understand it.[2] Coetzee's lectures themselves take the form of a story. In the story, an elderly woman novelist, Elizabeth Costello, has been invited to give an endowed lecture at Appleton College. She is a woman haunted by the horror of what we do to animals. We see her as wounded by this knowledge, this horror, and by the knowledge of how unhaunted others are. The wound marks her and isolates her. The imagery of the

Holocaust figures centrally in the way she is haunted, and in her isolation. For thinking this horror with the imagery of the Holocaust is or can be felt to be profoundly offensive.[3]

I want to describe Coetzee's lectures, then, as presenting a kind of woundedness or hauntedness, a terrible rawness of nerves. What wounds this woman, what haunts her mind,[4] is what we do to animals. This, in all its horror, is there, in our world. How is it possible to live in the face of it? And in the face of the fact that, for nearly everyone, it is as nothing, as the mere accepted background of life? Elizabeth Costello gives a lecture, but it is a lecture that distances itself in various ways from the expectations of a lecture audience. She describes herself as an animal exhibiting but not exhibiting, to a gathering of scholars, a wound which her clothes cover up, but which is touched on in every word she speaks. So the life of this speaking and wounded and clothed animal is one of the 'lives of animals' that the story is about; if it is true that we generally remain ✓ unaware of the lives of other animals, it is also true that, as readers of this story, we may remain unaware, as her audience does, of the life of the speaking animal at its center.

I say that that is how I want to describe Coetzee's lectures; but it is not how the commentators on the lectures describe them. Amy Gutmann, in her introductory essay, sees Coetzee as confronting the ethical issue how human beings should treat animals, and as presenting, within a fictional frame, arguments which are meant to support one way of resolving that issue. Peter Singer also reads Coetzee as having been engaged in the presenting of arguments within the frame of a fiction, arguments for a kind of 'radical egalitarianism' (91) as the appropriate way to organize our relations to animals. He thinks the arguments in Coetzee's lectures are not really very good ones, since they fail to make clear the source of the moral significance of the lives of animals.[5] The fact that the arguments are those of a character in a story he sees as simply making it possible for Coetzee to distance himself to some degree from them and to avoid taking full intellectual responsibility for them. Another one of the commentators, Wendy Doniger, takes the lectures to be deeply moving, but begins her response by attempting to identify the ideas implicit in the lectures. She reads the implicit idea as an argument from the appropriate emotions towards animals and emotional bonds with them to conclusions about appropriate actions towards them. And Barbara Smuts, a primatologist, describes the Coetzee lectures as a text containing a 'discourse on animal rights'.

For this kind of reading, the wounded woman, the woman with the haunted mind and the raw nerves, has no significance except as a device for putting forward (in an imaginatively stirring way) ideas about the resolution of a range of ethical issues, ideas which can then be abstracted and examined. For none of the commentators does the title of the story have any particular significance in relation to the wounded animal that the story has as its central character. For none of the commentators does the title of the story have any significance in how we might understand the story in relation to our own lives, the lives of the animals we are.

So we have then two quite different ways of seeing the lectures: as centrally concerned with the presenting of a wounded woman, and as centrally concerned with the presenting of a position on the issue how we should treat animals. The difference between the two readings comes out especially sharply if we consider the references to the Holocaust, references which are of immense significance in Coetzee's lectures. Gutmann treats them as a use by Coetzee of an argument from analogy.[6] Singer also treats the Holocaust imagery as playing a role in the argumentative structure which he reads in the lectures. He sees the references to the Holocaust as part of the argument by Elizabeth Costello for her brand of radical egalitarianism. There would, he believes, be nothing illegitimate in arguing that both the behavior of the Nazis towards the Jews and the world's response, or failure of response, to it have some points of resemblance to our treatment of animals and our failures to attend to what we do to animals. But the problem he sees with Elizabeth Costello's argument is that she equates the cases, which ignores the differences in moral significance between killing human beings and killing animals.[7]

Gutmann and Singer, then, take the Holocaust imagery in the lectures as constituting part of an argument. That there is a woman haunted by the Holocaust as it seems to be replaying itself in our lives with animals, that there is a wounded woman exhibiting herself as wounded through talk of the Holocaust that she knows will offend and not be understood—this drops totally away in Singer's reading and almost totally in Gutmann's. Gutmann does consider the presence in the text of a character, Abraham Stern, who takes Elizabeth Costello's use of the Holocaust to verge on blasphemy; Gutmann sees the presence of Stern as enabling Coetzee to represent the difficulties we may have in understanding each other's perspectives. But 'perspective' is too general and bland a term for the rawness of nerves we have in both Stern and Costello, in contrast with the unjangled, unraw nerves of the other characters. The contrast is made sharply present through Costello's own allusion to one of the most searing poems about the Holocaust, with its image of the human being in the ash in the air, as part of her portrayal of how we protect ourselves with a dullness or deadness of soul.[8] (Gutmann describes Stern as Costello's 'academic equal', but they are better seen as equals rather in the way their rawnervedness propels them towards or beyond the borders of academic decorum.)

The difference between the two contrasting types of readings concerns also the question whether Coetzee's lectures can simply be taken to be concerned with a moral or ethical issue. Or, rather, this isn't a question at all for one of the two kinds of readings: neither Gutmann nor Singer considers whether there is any problem in taking the lectures that way, which is the way they themselves understand discourse about 'animal rights'.[9] Of course, Coetzee's lectures might indeed be intended to grapple with that ethical issue; but since he has a character in the story he tells, for whom it is as problematic to treat this supposed 'issue' as an 'ethical issue' for serious discussion as it is problematic to treat Holocaust denial as an issue for serious discussion, one can hardly, I think, take for granted that the lectures can be read as concerned with that 'issue', and as providing arguments bearing on it. If we see in the lectures a wounded woman, one thing that wounds her is precisely the common and taken-for-granted mode of thought that 'how we should treat animals' is an 'ethical issue', and the knowledge that she will be taken to be contributing, or intending to contribute, to discussion of it. But what kind of beings are we for whom this is an 'issue'? (It is important here that the lectures bring us to the writings of Jonathan Swift and to questions about reading Swift, while none of the commentators except Garber even mentions Swift, or takes the pages devoted to Swift to be significant in their reconstruction of what Coetzee is concerned to do.[10])

Elizabeth Costello says that she doesn't want to be taken to be joining in the tradition of argumentation. She is letting us see her as what she is. She is someone immensely conscious of the limits of thinking, the limits of understanding, in the face of all that she is painfully aware of (45). So what then is the role of the argument-fragments which are contained in the Coetzee lectures? My comments on this are inconclusive, but are meant to reflect the idea that we cannot understand their role in Coetzee's lectures without first taking seriously how argument is treated within the story, by Elizabeth Costello. She does not engage with others in argument, in the sense in which philosophers do. Her responses to arguments from others move out from the kind of engagement in argument that might have been expected. She comments on the arguments put to her, but goes on from them in directions which suggest her own very different mode of approach. She does not take seriously the conventions of argumentation of a philosophy text, as comes out in her image of the dead hen speaking in the writings of Camus on the guillotine. (This is clearly, from the point of view of the conventions of argumentation, no way to respond to the argumentative point that animals cannot speak for themselves and claim rights for themselves as we can. The image itself is reminiscent of Wittgenstein's image of the rose having teeth in the mouth of the cow that chews up its food and dungs the rose.) Elizabeth

Costello's responses to arguments can be read as 'replies' in the philosophical sense only by ignoring important features of the story, in particular the kind of weight that such responses have in Costello's thought. In the life of the animal she is, argument does not have the weight we may take it to have in the life of the kind of animal we think of ourselves as being. She sees our reliance on argumentation as a way we may make unavailable to ourselves our own sense of what it is to be a living animal.[11] And she sees poetry, rather than philosophy, as having the capacity to return us to such a sense of what animal life is.[12] (Another way of trying to confront the issues here: to think of Coetzee's lectures as contributing to the 'debate' on how to treat animals is to fail to see how 'debate' as we understand it may have built into it a distancing of ourselves from our sense of our own bodily life and our capacity to respond to and to imagine the bodily life of others.)

I am not sure how helpful it is to say "Coetzee's lectures have to be read first of all as literature", because it is not clear what is meant by reading them as literature. But what is meant not to be done is at least somewhat clear: not pulling out ideas and arguments as if they had been simply clothed in fictional form as a way of putting them before us. (This is perhaps particularly clear in connection with the use of Holocaust imagery, where the desire to see the point being made by Coetzee by using the imagery leads to various formulations of the point in general terms: Coetzee is making clear the question whether there is any way of resolving ethical conflicts in cases in which people's sensibilities are far apart (Gutmann); or he is engaged in putting forward an argument, which he himself may or may not accept, for radical egalitarianism (Singer).—Elizabeth Costello asks herself, at the end of the story, whether she is making a mountain out of a molehill. The mind does, though, have mountains; has frightful no-man-fathomed cliffs: "Hold them cheap may who ne'er hung there". What is it like to hang there? What comfort is offered by her son? "There, there, it will soon be over"? "Here! creep, wretch, under a comfort serves in a whirlwind: all life death does end and each day dies with sleep." If we do not see how the Holocaust imagery gives a sense of what it is to hang on these cliffs, what it is to have nothing but the comfort of sleep and death in the face of what it is to hang on those cliffs, it seems to me we have not begun really to read the lectures. But it equally seems we may be driven, or take ourselves to be driven, to such a reading by philosophy, as we hear it pressing on us the insistent point that that portrayal is simply the portrayal, however moving it may be, of a subjective response, the significance of which needs to be examined.)

If we take as central in our reading the view Coetzee gives us of a profound disturbance of the soul, it may seem natural to go on to suggest something like this:

We can learn from the 'sick soul' how to see reality, as William James said in his Gifford Lectures. The 'sick soul' in the Coetzee lectures lets us see one of the difficulties of reality, the difficulty of human life in its relation to that of animals, of the horror of what we do, and the horror of our blotting it out of consciousness.

The trouble with that view of what we may learn from the lectures is that it is fixed entirely on Elizabeth Costello's view, and implicitly identifies it as Coetzee's. But he shows us also that her understanding of our relation to animals seems to throw into shadow the full horror of what we do to each other, as if we could not keep in focus the Holocaust as an image for what we do to animals without losing our ability to see *it*, and to see fully what it shows us of ourselves. So there is a part of the difficulty of reality here that is not seen by Costello: so far as we keep one sort of difficulty in view we seem blocked from seeing another. And there is also a further important theme of the lectures which we cannot get into view so long as we stay entirely with her understanding, the difficulty of attempting to bring a difficulty of reality into focus, in that any such attempt is inextricably intertwined with relations of power between people. Elizabeth Costello responds to the allegations that dietary restrictions, and arguments in favor of them, are a way of allowing some group of people to claim superiority over others; but the lectures themselves leave us with a picture of complex dynamics within her family, in which her grandchildren's responsiveness to animals and to eating baby animals cannot be pulled apart from the mutual resentment between her and her daughter-in-law.

Elizabeth Costello, talking about Ted Hughes, says that writers teach us more than they are aware of; writing about Wolfgang Koehler, she says that the book we read is not the book he thought he was writing. Garber says that we can take both remarks to be about Coetzee, but she then more or less drops the point. I would pick it up and use it this way: Coetzee gives us a view of a profound disturbance of soul, and puts that view into a complex context. What is done by doing so he cannot tell us, he does not know. What response we may have to the difficulties of the lectures, the difficulties of reality, is not something the lectures themselves are meant to settle. This itself expresses a mode of understanding of the kind of animal we are, and indeed of the moral life of this kind of animal.

III. DEFLECTION

I have suggested that Coetzee's lectures present a mode of understanding of the kind of animal we are, where that understanding can be present in poetry, in a broad sense of the term. There is also the idea that

Cavell

an understanding of the kind of animal we are is present only in a diminished and distorted way in philosophical argumentation. Philosophy characteristically misrepresents both our own reality and that of others, in particular those 'others' who are animals. What we then see in the response to Coetzee's lectures by Gutmann and Singer (and to a lesser degree by Doniger and Smuts) is that the lectures are put into the context of argumentative discourse on moral issues. I want a term for what is going on here, which I shall take from Cavell, from "Knowing and Acknowledging". Cavell writes about the philosopher who begins (we imagine) from an appreciation of something appalling: that I may be suffering, and my suffering be utterly unknown or uncared about; "and that others may be suffering and I not know" (1969b: 247). But the philosopher's understanding is *deflected*; the issue becomes deflected, as the philosopher thinks it or rethinks it in the language of philosophical scepticism. And philosophical responses to that scepticism, e.g., demonstrations that it is confused, further deflect from the truth here (260). I shall return to Cavell's ideas; here I simply want the notion of deflection, for describing what happens when we are moved from the appreciation, or attempt at appreciation, of a difficulty of reality to a philosophical or moral problem apparently in the vicinity.

Let me go back briefly to my first example, the poem from Ted Hughes. What is expressed there is the sense

the difficulty

of a difficulty that pushes us beyond what we can think. To attempt to think it is to feel one's thinking come unhinged. Our concepts, our ordinary life with our concepts, pass by this difficulty as if it were not there; the difficulty, if we try to see it, shoulders us out of life, is deadly chilling. How then can we describe the philosophical deflection from a difficulty of reality, as we see it in Gutmann and Singer? I have in mind centrally their taking Coetzee as contributing to the discussion of a moral issue: how we should treat animals. Should we eat them, should we grant them rights? And so on. Philosophy knows how to do this. It is hard, all right, but that is what university philosophy departments are for, to enable us to learn how to discuss hard problems, what constitutes a good argument, what is distorted by emotion, when we are making assertions without backing them up. What I have meant to suggest by picking up Cavell's use of the term 'deflection' is that the hardness there, in philosophical argumentation, is not the hardness of appreciating or trying to appreciate a difficulty of reality. In the latter case, the difficulty lies in the apparent resistance by reality to one's ordinary mode of life, including one's ordinary modes of thinking: to appreciate the difficulty is to feel oneself being shouldered out of how one thinks, how one is apparently supposed to think, or to have a sense of the inability of thought to encompass what it is attempting to reach. Such appreciation may involve the profound isolation felt by someone like Elizabeth Costello. Recall here her reference to her body as wounded: her isolation is felt in the body, as the speaker in Hughes's poem feels a bodily thrownness from the photograph. Coetzee's lectures ask us to inhabit a body.[13] But, just as, in considering what death is to an animal we may reject our own capacity to inhabit its body in imagination,[14] so we may, in reading the lectures, reject our own capacity to inhabit in imagination the body of the woman confronting, trying to confront, the difficulty of what we do to animals. The deflection into discussion of a moral issue is a deflection which makes our own bodies mere facts—facts which may or may not be thought of as morally relevant in this or that respect, depending on the particular moral issue being addressed (as our sentience, for example, might be taken to be relevant to our having 'moral status'). So here I am inviting you to think of what it would be not to be 'deflected' as an inhabiting of a body (one's own, or an imagined other's) in the appreciating of a difficulty of reality. This may make it sound as if philosophy is inevitably deflected from appreciation of the kind of difficulty I mean, if (that is) philosophy does not know how to inhabit a body (does not know how to treat a wounded body as anything but a fact). I shall return to that question later, and also to Coetzee on imagining one's own death, on having a genuinely embodied knowledge of being extinguished. For that is another important point in the lectures, not mentioned by any of the commentators.

IV. BEAUTY AND GOODNESS, AND SPIKINESS

I said at the beginning that I was concerned with a range of phenomena; and so far I have had only two examples, which cannot by themselves adequately suggest the range. I want briefly to mention some other examples to go a part of the way to remedying that.

My first example involved a poem about life and death; the second example involved the horror of what we do to animals. But I would include in what I call the difficulty of reality some things that are entirely different. Instances of goodness or of beauty can throw us. I mean that they can give us the sense that *this* should not be, that we cannot fit it into the understanding we have of what the world is like. It is wholly inexplicable that it should be; and yet it is. That is what Czeslaw Milosz writes about beauty: "It should not exist. There is not only no reason for it, but an argument against. Yet undoubtedly it is . . ." And he writes of the mystery that may seem to be present in the architecture of a tree, the slimness of a column crowned with green, or in the voices of birds outside the window greeting the morning. How can this be?—In the case of our relationship with animals, a sense of the difficulty of reality may involve not only the kind of horror felt by

Elizabeth Costello in Coetzee's lectures, but also and equally a sense of astonishment and incomprehension that there should be beings so like us, so unlike us, so astonishingly capable of being companions of ours and so unfathomably distant. A sense of its being impossible that we should go and *eat* them may go with feeling how powerfully strange it is that they and we should share as much as we do, and yet also not share; that they should be capable of incomparable beauty and delicacy and terrible ferocity; that some among them should be so mind-bogglingly weird or repulsive in their forms or in their lives. Later I will come to Cavell's remarks about human separateness as turned equally toward splendor and toward horror, mixing beauty and ugliness, but those words, which he calls on to help give the felt character of human separateness, are very like words we might call on to express the extraordinary felt character of animal life in relation to our own.

Ruth Klüger, in her memoir *Still Alive: A Holocaust Girlhood Remembered*, describes her own astonishment and awe at the act of the young woman at Auschwitz who first encouraged a terrified child, Ruth at 12, to tell a lie that might help save her life, and who then stood up for her, got her through a selection. Klüger says that she tells the story in wonder, that she has never ceased to wonder at that girl's doing, the "incomparable and inexplicable" goodness that touched her that day (103–109). In discussing Hughes's poem, I mentioned that the photograph and what it shows would not be taken to boggle the mind by everyone. The men were alive, and now are dead; what's the problem? Klüger says that when she tells her story in wonder,

> people wonder at my wonder. They say, okay, some persons are altruistic. We understand that; it doesn't surprise us. The girl who helped you was one of those who liked to help.

Here, as in the case of the Hughes poem, what is capable of astonishing one in its incomprehensibility, its not being fittable in with the world as one understands it, may be seen by others as unsurprising. Klüger asks her readers not just to look at the scene but to listen to her and not take apart what happened, to "absorb it" as she tells it (108–109). She asks for a kind of imagination that can inhabit her own continued astonishment. The 'taking apart' that she asks us to eschew would be a distancing from the story, a fitting of what went on into this or that way of handling things, a deflecting from the truth.

(In a discussion of concepts of the miraculous, R. F. Holland sets out one such concept as that of the occurrence of something which is at one and the same time empirically certain and conceptually impossible. The story in the New Testament of water having been turned into wine is "the story of something that could have been known empirically to have occurred, and it is also the story of the occurrence of something which is conceptually impossible". To be the miracle story it is, Holland says, it has to be both; the sort of occurrence he means is one which, for us, is impossible to think, and yet it is there. Klüger, in introducing the story of what happened to her, describes it as an act of grace, and I do not want to suggest that that is the same as seeing it as a miracle, in Holland's sense. But I do want to connect the astonishment and awe that Klüger expresses as related to the astonishment and awe that one would feel at a miracle in Holland's sense, and indeed to the astonishment Milosz expresses at the existence of beauty.)

Mary Mann's story, "Little Brother", is described by A. S. Byatt (in her introductory essay for the *Oxford Book of English Short Stories*) as "plain, and brief, and clear and terrible". Mann's telling of the story is "spiky with morals and the inadequacy of morals". Byatt says no more than that; and it is therefore not entirely obvious what she means by the telling's being spiky with the inadequacy of morals, and how that is related to the terribleness of what is related. (What is related is the playing of two poor children, who have no toys, with the corpse of their newborn, stillborn brother. His stiff little body is the only doll they have had. The narrator had told the mother what she thought of the desecration;

the last word is given to the mother.) The telling, fully felt, shoulders us from a familiar sense of moral life, from a sense of being able to take in and think a moral world. Moral thought gets no grip here. The terribleness of what is going on and the terribleness of the felt resistance of the narrated reality to moral thought are inseparable. (A story which seems to me comparable in its 'spikiness' with morals and the inadequacy of morals is Leonard Woolf's "Pearls and Swine". On one level, the story is a criticism of racism and colonialism; but it is also a telling of the kind of terribleness that, fully felt, shoulders one from one's familiar sense of moral life.) Again here I should want to note that the sense of this or another narrated reality as resisting our modes of moral thought is not something everyone would recognize.

V. TURNED TO STONE

Hughes's poem again: The contradictory permanent horrors shoulder out one's body from its instant and heat. To look is to experience death, to be turned to stone. Losing one's instant and heat, being turned to something permanent and hard and cold, is a central image in Cavell's discussion of scepticism and knowledge in *The Winter's Tale* and *Othello* (1979: 481–96). He says of *Winter's Tale* that Hermione's fate of being turned to stone can be understood as her undergoing what is in a sense the fate of Leontes. Leontes's failure or inability to recognize her makes her as stone; "hence", Cavell says, that is what it does to him. "One can see this as the projection of his own sense of numbness, of living death"; and Cavell then asks why that was Leontes's fate (481). Cavell links the two plays with a play on words: in both plays, "the consequence for the man's refusal of knowledge of his other is an imagination of stone": stone as what is imagined and stoniness as what has befallen the imagination. Othello imagines Desdemona's skin as having the smoothness of alabaster (481–2). He imagines her as stone, says that she stones her heart. It is Othello, though, who "will give her a stone heart for her stone body"; his "words of stone" transfer to her what he himself has undergone, a heart turned to stone (492). What does this to Othello is the intolerableness to him of Desdemona's existence, her separateness. About the possibility of that separateness Cavell says that it is precisely what tortures Othello: "The content of his torture is the premonition of the existence of another, hence of his own, his own as dependent, as partial." (493) Separateness can be felt as horror;[15] such a response is what puts Othello "beyond aid".

Cavell has in many of his writings traced connections and relations between on the one hand the multifarious forms in which we take in or try to take in or resist taking in that difficulty of reality that he refers to most often as separateness and on the other hand scepticism: scepticism as itself both a presence in our lives and as, intellectualized, a central part of our philosophical tradition. The early direction his thoughts took on these issues can be seen in his statement of one form of the 'conclusion' towards which he took those thoughts to be heading, that "skepticism concerning other minds is not skepticism but is tragedy".[16] Earlier still, he had been particularly concerned, in "Knowing and Acknowledging" (1969b), with what he took to be inadequate in the Wittgensteinian response to scepticism: I mean the response of such Wittgensteinians as Norman Malcolm and John Cook, not that of Wittgenstein. Malcolm and Cook had taken the sceptic about other minds to be confused about what can be said in the language-game in which we speak about our own sensations and those of others, in which we express our own feelings and in which we may speak of what we know of the feelings of others, what we doubt or are certain of. Thus Cook (1965) had criticized the idea that it is some sort of limitation on us that we cannot actually feel what another person feels, cannot have that very feeling; such an idea reflects (he thinks) one's taking the inaccessibility of the feeling as like the inaccessibility of a flower in a garden on the far side of a wall over which one cannot see. What Cook was criticizing was the idea I may have of the position that I cannot be in in respect to the pain of the other person, the position that that person himself is in, the decisive position. His argument was an attempt to show that the sceptic takes to be a kind of inability what is really a matter of the difference between two language-games: in the language-game with pain, there is no such thing as the position in which one has *that which* the other person has. We are not 'unable' to be *there* if there is no there where we are unable to be. Cook's account was thus meant to enable us to see the confusion in the sceptic's view. Cavell's response was astonishing. He places Cook's argument in the situation from which the sceptic speaks; leads us to imagine that situation and to recognize the pressures on words; shows us what may happen with our experience of distance from what others undergo. When we put, or try to put, that experience in words, the words fail us, the words don't do what we are trying to get them to do. The words make it look as if I am simply unable to see over a wall which happens to separate me from something I want very much to see. But the fact that the words are apparently too weak to do what I am demanding from them does not mean that the experience here of *powerlessness* has been shown to involve a kind of grammatical error. But why, then, since words seem not to be able to do what I want, did I call on them? Why, in particular, does the experience appear to be an experience of not being able to know what is there in the other because I cannot have what he has? Cavell says ". . . I am filled with this feeling—of our separateness, let us say—and

I want you to have it too. So I give voice to it. And then my powerlessness presents itself as ignorance—a metaphysical finitude as an intellectual lack". (1969b: 263) His criticism of Cook, then, takes the form of allowing us to hear Cook's own voice differently. When Cook, in repudiating the sceptic's idea, speaks of it as 'inherently confused', Cavell lets us hear his voice as responding with 'correctness' to the voice of philosophical scepticism.[17] When I spoke of Cavell's response as astonishing, I meant his teaching us a way of hearing both Cook and the sceptic whom he is criticizing, a way of hearing these voices that puts them back into the situation within which the humanness of the other seems out of reach, and thereby shows us where and how philosophy has to start.—This takes us back to the subject of deflection.

In Part III, I quoted Cavell's description of how we may be filled with a sense of the facts, the ineluctable facts of our capacity to miss the suffering of others and of the possibility of our own suffering being unknown and uncared about; we may be filled with a sense of these facts, of our distance from each other, and our appreciation be deflected, the problem itself be deflected, into one or another of the forms it is given in philosophical scepticism. I quoted also Cavell's remark about the anti-sceptical response as a further deflection, a deflection that ignores the fundamental insight of the sceptic (1969b: 258–60), the sense the sceptic has of the other's position with respect to his own pain, and the light in which it casts his position in relation to that other. The image of deflection is implicit also later on in Cavell's writings, when he describes the difficulty of philosophy as that of not being able to find and stay on a path (*New Yet Unapproachable America*, 1989: 37); for we can here see deflection as deflection from a path we need to find and stay on; but it is also deflection from seeing, deflection from taking in, the tormenting possibility central to the experience of the sceptic. What he sees of the human condition, what unseats his reason, is converted into and treated as an intellectual difficulty (1979: 493). I shall come back to this, but first I want to make further connections with Coetzee's lectures and Hughes's poem.

VI. CORRECTNESS AND EXPOSURE

There is in Coetzee's second lecture a response by a fictional philosopher, Thomas O'Hearne, to Elizabeth Costello's ideas (1999: 59–65). It is implicitly a response also to some of the arguments in favor of animal rights put forward by philosophers like Singer and Tom Regan. But here I want to consider a response by a real philosopher, Michael Leahy, a response which has some resemblances to O'Hearne's but which will more easily enable us to see the connections with Cavell's thought. Leahy's argument has two parts. He first tries to establish what the language-game is within which we speak of animals and their pains and desires and so on.[18] His argument is that animal liberationists characteristically fail to recognize that the language-game in which we speak of the mental life of animals, of a dog fearing this or a chimpanzee believing that, is "vitally different" from the language-game in which we use such terms of human beings (138–9). Leahy relies on that point when he goes on to argue that the practices within which we use animals in various ways (as pets, food, experimental subjects, sources of fur and so on) "dictate the criteria for our judging what constitutes needless suffering" (198), and that is the second part of the overall argument. The two parts of his argument together are thus meant to undercut the case made for animal rights. Leahy's response to the liberationists is not unlike Cook's response to scepticism about other minds: like Cook, he takes the failure to recognize the difference between distinct language-games to be the ultimate source of the confusion he wants to diagnose. There are various questions that might be raised about how the two parts of his argument are connected, about whether the recognition of the differences between the language-games has the practical implications that Leahy thinks it has.[19] But that is not my concern here. I am interested rather in Leahy's voice, and its relation to the anti-sceptical voice exemplified for Cavell in "Knowing and Acknowledging" by the voices of Malcolm and Cook. The Coetzee case is not an exact parallel to Cavell's; and the philosophical debates about animals cannot be treated as more than partially parallel to the debate about scepticism.[20] But we are concerned in both cases with a repudiation of the everyday; with a sense of being shouldered out from our ways of thinking and speaking by a torment of reality. In both cases, the repudiation may be heard as expressing such-and-such position in an intellectualized debate; in both cases, the opposite sides in the debate may have more in common than they realize. In the voices we hear in the debate about animal rights, those of people like Singer on the one hand and those of Leahy and the fictional O'Hearne on the other, there is shared a desire for a 'because': because animals are this kind of being, or because they are that kind of being, thus-and-such is their standing for our moral thought. If we listen to these voices in the way Cavell has taught us to, can we hear in them a form of scepticism? That is, a form of scepticism in the desire for something better than what we are condemned to (as the kind of animal we are)? But what might we be thought to be 'condemned to'? Cavell, in *The Claim of Reason*, uses the word 'exposure' in discussing our situation: Being exposed, as I am in the case of 'my concept of the other', means that my assurance in applying the concept isn't provided for me. "The other can present me with no mark or feature on the basis of which I can *settle* my attitude"

(433). He says that to accept my exposure, in the case of my knowledge of others, "seems to imply an acceptance of the possibility that my knowledge of others may be overthrown, even that it ought to be"; it implies acceptance of not being in what I may take to be the ideal position, what I want or take myself to want (439; see also 454). Our 'exposure' in the case of animals lies in there being nothing but our own responsibility, our own making the best of it. We are not, here too, in what we might take to be the 'ideal' position. We want to be able to see that, given what animals are, and given also our properties, what we are like (given our 'marks and features' and theirs), there are general principles that establish the moral significance of their suffering compared to ours, of their needs compared to ours, and we could then see what treatment of them was and what was not morally justified. We would be *given* the presence or absence of moral community (or thus-and-such degree or kind of moral community) with animals. But we are exposed—that is, we are thrown into finding something we can live with, and it may at best be a kind of bitter-tasting compromise. There is here only what we make of our exposure, and it leaves us endless room for double-dealing and deceit. The exposure is most plain in the Coetzee lectures at the point at which Elizabeth Costello is asked whether her vegetarianism comes out of moral conviction, and replies that it doesn't; "It comes out of a desire to save my soul", and she adds that she is wearing leather shoes, and carrying a leather purse.[21]

The title of this essay is "The difficulty of reality and the difficulty of philosophy", but a word I'd want to add to the title is: *exposure*. Ted Hughes's poem is about *a single exposure*, but the single exposure is *our* exposure, as we find for ourselves, or are meant to find, in a shuddering awareness of death and life together. In the background is perhaps a reference to Wilfred Owen's "Exposure", in which the sense of war as not making sense, the sense of loss of sense, is tied to death literally by exposure, exposure to cold that transforms the men to iced solidity.—I have not more than scratched the surface of Cavell's use of the idea of exposure; but there is also more to the idea in Coetzee's lectures. Elizabeth Costello, in Coetzee's first lecture, speaks of her own knowledge of death, in a passage which (in the present context) takes us to the "contradictory permanent horrors" spoken of in Hughes's poem. "For an instant at a time", she says, "I know what it is like to be a corpse. The knowledge repels me. It fills me with terror; I shy away from it, refuse to entertain it." She goes on to say that we all have such moments, and that the knowledge we then have is not abstract but embodied. "For a moment we *are* that knowledge. We live the impossible: we live beyond our death, look back on it, yet look back as only a dead self can". She goes on, making the contradiction explicit: "What I know is what a corpse cannot know: that it is extinct, that it knows nothing and will never know anything anymore. For an instant, before my whole structure of knowledge collapses in panic, I am alive inside that contradiction, dead and alive at the same time" (32). The awareness we each have of being a living body, being "alive to the world", carries with it exposure to the bodily sense of vulnerability to death, sheer animal vulnerability, the vulnerability we share with them. This vulnerability is capable of panicking us. To be able to acknowledge it at all, let alone as shared, is wounding; but acknowledging it as shared with other animals, in the presence of what we do to them, is capable not only of panicking one but also of isolating one, as Elizabeth Costello is isolated. Is there any difficulty in seeing why we should not prefer to return to moral debate, in which the livingness and death of animals enter as facts that we treat as relevant in this or that way, not as presences that may unseat our reason?

VII. THE DIFFICULTY OF PHILOSOPHY

Can there be such a thing as philosophy that is not deflected from such realities?[22] This is a great question for Simone Weil. She wrote

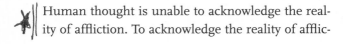

Human thought is unable to acknowledge the reality of affliction. To acknowledge the reality of affliction means saying to oneself: "I may lose at any moment, through the play of circumstances over which I have no control, anything whatsoever that I possess, including those things which are so intimately mine that I consider them as being myself. There is nothing that I might not lose. It could happen at any moment that what I am might be abolished and replaced by anything whatsoever of the filthiest and most contemptible sort."

To be aware of this in the depth of one's soul is to experience non-being. (1986: 70)

Weil's writings show that she saw the difficulty of what she was doing as the difficulty of keeping to such awareness, of not being deflected from it. I give her as an example of a philosopher concerned with deflection from the difficulty of reality, but a philosopher very different from Cavell.

In the concluding two paragraphs of *The Claim of Reason*, Cavell speaks of Othello and Desdemona, lying dead.

A statue, a stone, is something whose existence is fundamentally open to the ocular proof. A human being is not. The two bodies lying together form an emblem of this fact, the truth of skepticism. What this man lacked was not certainty. He knew everything, but he could not yield to what he knew, be

commanded by it. He found out too much for his
mind, not too little. Their differences from one another—the one everything the other is not—form
an emblem of human separation, which can be accepted, and granted, or not.   (1979: 496)

Cavell returns to the audience: "we are here, knowing
they are 'gone burning to hell'. He asks: ". . . can philosophy accept them back at the hands of poetry?", and
answers, "Certainly not so long as philosophy continues, as it has from the first, to demand the banishment
of poetry from its republic. Perhaps it could if it could
itself become literature. But can philosophy become
literature and still know itself?"

What follows is not meant to answer that last question, but to bear on it.

It may seem as if Cavell is here taking for granted
that literature can accept—no problem!—such realities
as throw philosophy. I do not think that that is an implication, but I won't discuss it.[23] I want to look instead
at Cavell's question whether philosophy can accept
Othello and Desdemona back, at the hands of poetry.
For philosophy to do so would be for philosophy to accept human separateness as "turned equally toward
splendor and toward horror, mixing beauty and ugliness; turned toward before and after; toward flesh and
blood"; for philosophy not to accept them back is for
philosophy not to get near, but to get deflected from, the

forms which our exposure to that separateness takes. But if that suggests a conception of the difficulty of philosophy, the difficulty of staying turned toward before and after, toward flesh and blood, towards the life of the animals we are, how is it related to what Cavell says elsewhere about the difficulty of philosophy?

In "Notes and Afterthoughts on the Opening of Wittgenstein's *Investigations*", Cavell says that the medium of philosophy, as Wittgenstein understands it, "lies in demonstrating, or say showing, the obvious"; he then asks how the obvious can fail to be obvious. What is the hardness of seeing the obvious?—And he then says that this must bear on what the hardness of philosophizing is. (1996: 271–2) This question is present also in his reflections on Wittgenstein's aim of bringing words back from their metaphysical to their everyday use. What can the difficulty be, then, of bringing or leading words back? What is the everyday, if it is so hard to achieve? It is within the everyday that there lie the forms and varieties of repudiation of our language-games and distance from them, the possibility of being tormented by the hiddenness, the separateness, the otherness of others (1989: passim). As a form of repudiation of the language-game in which there is no contradiction between the young men being profoundly alive and then totally dead may be in the life of the Hughes poem; which is itself not to be thought of as outside life with the words we use for thinking of life and death.

In Part I, when I introduced the phrase "a difficulty of reality", I said that, in the cases I had in mind, the reality to which we were attending seemed to resist our thinking it. That our thought and reality might fail to meet is itself the content of a family of forms of scepticism, to which one response is that the very idea of such a failure is confused, that what I have spoken of as the content of such forms of scepticism is not a content at all. A language, a form of thought, cannot (we may be told) get things right or wrong, fit or fail to fit reality; it can only be more or less useful. What I want to end with is not exactly a response to that: it is to note how much that coming apart of thought and reality belongs to flesh and blood. I take that, then, to be itself a thought joining Hughes, Coetzee, and Cavell.

NOTES

This paper was presented at a symposium, "Accounting for Literary Language", at the University of East Anglia in September 2002, and at the Hannah Arendt/Reiner Schürmann Memorial Symposium, on Stanley Cavell, held at the New School in New York, in October 2002. I am very grateful for the comments of the audience on both occasions. I was helped to think about the issues by Anat Matar's reply to my paper at the conference in East Anglia. I am also very glad to have had comments and suggestions from Alice Crary and Talbot Brewer.

The paper was originally published in *Partial Answers*, vol. 1 (2003), and I am grateful for many suggestions and careful editorial attention from Leona Toker and her assistants.

1. I believe I read it in a *New Yorker* essay of his in the 1980s, but cannot trace it.

2. The two Coetzee Lectures have been reprinted as Lessons 3 and 4 in Coetzee 2003.

3. The description of her as 'haunted' has, for me in this context, two particular sources. One is Ruth Klüger's discussion of Sylvia Plath and of Plath's use of Holocaust imagery in her poetry, her defence of Plath against those who object to her taking over what has happened to us, to the Jews, in expressing a private despair. (She was writing about Alvin Rosenfeld in particular, but had in mind others who shared his view, and who felt as he did that there was an 'unforgivable disproportion' in Plath's expression of her own anguish in language drawing on the Holocaust. See her 1985, especially 184–5.) Klüger speaks of how 'others' (other than we who ask the world to remember what happened to us) may be "haunted by what has happened to the Jews and claim it as their own out of human kinship, as part of their private terrors and visions of death". The second source is Coetzee's story, in which Elizabeth Costello mentions Camus and the haunting imprint on his memory made by the death-cry of a hen, which, as a little boy, he had fetched for his grandmother, who then beheaded it (63).

4. I use the word 'mind' here with some hesitation, since (within the context of discussion of animals and

ourselves) it may be taken to suggest a contrast with bodily life. Conceptions of mind are at stake within the lectures. In particular, there is involved a critical stance towards the idea that, if one were to imagine what it is like to be a bat or other animal, or to be another human being, one would need to imagine what is going on 'in its mind', rather than to imagine its fulness of being (see, e.g., 33, 51, 65). So, to speak of Elizabeth Costello as having a haunted mind in a sense of 'mind' which takes that understanding of embodiment seriously is to speak of how her life is felt.

5. 'Fail to make clear' is my way of putting the criticism; see Singer, 87–90. Singer's response doesn't take on Elizabeth Costello's rejection of the form of argument that Singer thinks is appropriate, argument which responds to the *therefore*-arguments of those who justify treating animals as we do by their own different *therefore*-arguments. She comments on such arguments after one of the other characters in the fiction speaks of the 'vacuum of consciousness' within which animals live (44). We say such things as that they have no consciousness, but what she minds is, she says, what comes next: "They have no consciousness *therefore*. Therefore what?". Against those who say that therefore we may treat them as we like, she does not reply that animals are conscious, *therefore* we may not eat them, or that they have other relevant properties, *therefore* we should recognize their rights, etc. See also below, note 12.

6. See "Introduction", 8. When she describes Coetzee as arguing by analogy, Gutmann is actually speaking

about Marjorie Garber's discussion of Coetzee's use of the Holocaust, but interestingly Garber herself, although she has quite a long discussion of the use of analogies by Coetzee and others, never refers to the cases in question as the presentation of a kind of argument. While I would disagree with Garber's reading, she does at any rate, unlike all the other commentators, begin by taking for granted that we have in front of us something to be thought about in literary terms, and that this matters.

7. I do not in this essay try to judge, or even to examine what would be involved in trying to judge, Elizabeth Costello's use of the imagery of the Holocaust. Later in the present section I do, though, discuss how the effort to take in one difficulty of reality may block us from seeing another.

8. I had meant Paul Celan's "Todesfuge"; I am indebted to Ruth Klüger for pointing out to me that Nelly Sachs makes use of that image too ("Dein Leib im Rauch durch die Luft").

9. See especially the opening paragraph of Gutmann's introduction, intended to help fix the terms of our reading of the rest of the book: the lectures, she says, focus on an important ethical issue—the way human beings treat animals; cf. also the following page, where that description is repeated.

10. I cannot here go into the discussion of Swift in Coetzee's lectures. It is important for various reasons, among which is that it takes up the question where we might get if we push Swift's tales further than we usually do, and suggests an 'ex-colonial' perspective on what,

thus pushed, the tales might say about the kind of being we are.

11. There is an issue here that I can merely indicate. I have found, in teaching undergraduates how utilitarians discuss the killing of babies, that my students react very strongly indeed to claims that killing a baby does not wrong the baby, that it does not interfere with what the baby might be taken to want for itself, since the baby is not as yet capable of grasping such a choice. Killing an older child might (on this view) go against what it wants, but that is possible only because the older child can understand what it is to go on living, and can therefore want to do so.—In response to that sort of argument, the students say that you are wronging the baby; that the baby is attached to life: In the struggle of a baby or animal whom someone is trying to kill, you can see that it is clinging to life. They reject the idea that there is no interference with what a baby or animal might be said to want. Their rejection of the utilitarian argument is connected with their rejection of the kind of argumentative discourse in which the utilitarian wants the issue cast, a form of discourse in which one's imaginative sense of what might be one's own bodily struggle for life, one's imaginative sense of an animal's struggle for life, cannot be given the role they want it to have. It is as if they felt a kind of evisceration of the meaning of 'wanting to go on living'.

12. Gutmann in fact does recognize some of the features of the lectures which I have just described, but takes Costello's responses to argument as showing that

she is after all willing to engage in argument to at least a limited degree. She speaks of Costello as employing philosophy in demonstrating the weakness of arguments opposed to her own view, but Gutmann's treatment of the argument-fragments which the story contains is shaped by her basic reading of the story as a way of presenting a stance on an ethical issue. My reading of the arguments in the Coetzee lectures would go in a different direction, and would focus on some of the specific cases, in particular Elizabeth Costello's rejection of the *therefore*-arguments that go from characteristics of animals to its therefore being permissible to treat them this or that way, as we do. Earlier I mentioned Singer's response to such arguments with contrasting *therefore*-arguments; a very different response that in some ways resembles Elizabeth Costello's is that of Rush Rhees, in "Humans and Animals: A Confused Christian Conception", which is not an essay but two sets of exploratory notes and a letter to a friend. A theme in the notes and in the letter is the unexamined use of *therefore*-arguments the conclusion of which is the supposed greater importance of human life; in fact a criticism of the '*therefore*' is the starting point of the first set of those notes, which characterize such arguments as reflecting "the illusion of a *reason* which justifies one in treating animals with less respect or less consideration than human beings". So a question for Rhees in these informal notes is how to think his own response to what he takes to be illusion.

13. See 51; here I am taking a remark of Elizabeth Costello's as deeply Coetzee's.

14. Central to the lectures: see 65; also 32. I return to this region of Coetzee's thought in Part VI.

15. Cavell says that human separateness is "turned equally toward splendor and toward horror, mixing beauty and ugliness; turned toward before and after; toward flesh and blood" (492). My discussion is partial at this point, emphasizing as it does horror over splendor. But see also 494–6.

16. Foreword to *Claim of Reason* (1979: xix). What Cavell says is more complex than my quotation: He says that he knew (in 1973 and 74) the direction that the conclusion of his work in progress was "hauling itself toward", and that that conclusion had to do with the connection of "Knowing and Acknowledging" and "The Avoidance of Love", "the reciprocation between the ideas of acknowledgment and of avoidance, for example as the thought that skepticism concerning other minds is not skepticism but is tragedy" (xviii–xix).

17. "Knowing and Acknowledging" (1969b: 259–60); the term 'voice of correctness' comes from Cavell's "Availability of Wittgenstein's Later Philosophy" (1969a: 71)

18. All of chapter 5 of *Against Liberation* (1991) is relevant, but p. 126 is particularly helpful in making clear Leahy's method and aims.

19. There are also questions about the first part of the argument, the attempt to establish the differences between the language-game in which we speak about the thoughts, feelings and intentions of animals and that in which we speak about our own. One question would concern the idea of there being just the two language-

games he describes. The question is particularly acute in connection with the writings of Vicki Hearne, which Leahy discusses and criticizes at various points in the book. One way of putting her understanding of what is involved in talking about animals is that talking about animals in connection with their 'work' (in her sense of that term) is itself a distinctive language-game. This language-game she takes to be inseparable from the trainer's activity; the activity itself is carried on through such talk, and the talk gets its sense through what it achieves in the shared 'work'. See, in addition to *Adam's Task* (Hearne, 1986, the target of Leahy's criticism), her essay "A Taxonomy of Knowing: Animals Captive, Free-Ranging, and at Liberty", (1995), 441–56.

20. For one thing, I don't want to suggest that Leahy's use of the concept of criteria in his argument is an appeal to criteria in Cavell's sense. But more important than that, there is a significant difference between the two cases in the conceptions of knowledge in play. The sort of knowledge to which Elizabeth Costello appeals when she discusses the attachment of animals to life can be contrasted with that which Othello takes himself to want. See, on knowledge and forms of perception in *Othello*, and on Othello's desire for proof, Naomi Scheman's "Othello's Doubt/Desdemona's Death: The Engendering of Skepticism", in *Pursuits of Reason*. Scheman's essay itself helps to bring out also a connection between the issues I have been discussing and issues concerning gender, both within Coetzee's lectures and more generally.

21. To forestall misunderstanding here, I want to note that I am not (in this section or anywhere else) denying a role, indeed a large and deeply significant role, to 'because' in moral thinking, and indeed to argument. I am suggesting we look with some serious puzzlement at attempts to establish moral community, or to show it to be absent, through attention to 'marks and features'.

22. Alice Crary has pointed out to me that my descriptions, earlier in this essay, of how philosophical argument can deflect us from attention to the difficulty of reality may seem to have implied the answer "No" to my question whether there can be a non-deflecting practice of philosophy. That there can be such a practice, and that argument may have an essential role in it, is not something I would wish to deny. There are here two distinct points: philosophical argument is not in and of itself any indication that attention has been or is being deflected from the difficulty of reality, and (more positively) philosophical argument has an important role to play in bringing to attention such difficulty and in exploring its character, as well as in making clear what the limits or limitations are of philosophical argument, and indeed of other argument. See, for example, Cavell's arguments about the argument that the human embryo is a human being (1979: 372–8).

23. The kinds of difficulty which literature may have in the face of a 'difficulty of reality' are emphasized by Simone Weil in remarks about the representation of affliction. See "Human Personality" (1986: 72).

WORKS CITED

Byatt, A. S. 1998. "Introduction". In A.S. Byatt, ed., *The Oxford Book of English Short Stories*. Oxford: Oxford University Press, pp. xv–xxx.

Cavell, Stanley. 1969a. "The Availability of Wittgenstein's Later Philosophy". In *Must We Mean What We Say?* New York: Scribner's, pp. 44–72.

——. 1969b. "Knowing and Acknowledging". In *Must We Mean What We Say?* New York: Scribner's, pp. 238–66.

——. 1979. *The Claim of Reason: Wittgenstein, Skepticism, Morality, and Tragedy*. Oxford: Clarendon Press.

——. 1989. "Declining Decline". In *This New Yet Unapproachable America: Lectures after Emerson after Wittgenstein*. Albuquerque: Living Batch Press, pp. 29–75.

——. 1996. "Notes and Afterthoughts on the Opening of Wittgenstein's *Investigations*". In Hans Sluga and David G. Stern, eds., *The Cambridge Companion to Wittgenstein*. Cambridge: Cambridge University Press, pp. 261–95.

Coetzee, J. M. 1999. *The Lives of Animals*. Ed. Amy Gutmann. Princeton: Princeton University Press.

——. 2003. *Elizabeth Costello*. New York: Viking.

Cook, John. 1965. "Wittgenstein on Privacy". *The Philosophical Review* 74: 281–314.

Doniger, Wendy. 1999. "Reflections". In Coetzee 1999: 93–106.

Garber, Marjorie. 1999. "Reflections". In Coetzee 1999: 73–84.

Gutmann, Amy. 1999. "Introduction". In Coetzee 1999: 3–11.

Hearne, Vicki. 1986. *Adam's Task: Calling Animals by Name*. New York: Knopf.

——. 1995. "A Taxonomy of Knowing: Animals Captive, Free-Ranging, and at Liberty". In *Social Research* 62: 441–56.

Holland, R. F. 1965. "The Miraculous". *American Philosophical Quarterly* 2: 43–51.

Hughes, Ted. 1957. "Six Young Men". In *The Hawk in the Rain*. London: Faber and Faber, pp. 54–55.

James, William. 1960. *Varieties of Religious Experience*. London: Collins.

Klüger, Ruth. (Angress, Ruth K.) 1985. "Discussing Holocaust Literature". *Simon Wiesenthal Center Annual* 2: 179–192.

——. 2001. *Still Alive: A Holocaust Girlhood Remembered*. New York: The Feminist Press at the City University of New York.

Mann, Mary. 1998. "Little Brother". In A. S. Byatt, ed., *The Oxford Book of English Short Stories*. Oxford: Oxford University Press, pp. 93–96.

Milosz, Czeslaw. 1988. "One More Day". In *The Collected Poems*. New York: Ecco, pp. 108–109.

Rhees, Rush. 1999. "Humans and Animals: A Confused Christian Conception". In *Moral Questions*. Basingstoke: Macmillan, pp. 189–96.

Scheman, Naomi. 1993. "Othello's Doubt/Desdemona's Death: The Engendering of Scepticism". In Ted Cohen, Paul Guyer and Hilary Putnam, eds., *Pursuits of Reason: Essays in Honor of Stanley Cavell*. Lubbock: Texas Tech University Press, pp. 161–76.

Singer, Peter. 1999. "Reflections". In Coetzee 1999: 85–91.

Smuts, Barbara. 1999. "Reflections". In Coetzee 1999: 107–120.

Weil, Simone. 1986. "Human Personality". In Siân Miles, ed., *Simone Weil: An Anthology*. New York: Weidenfeld and Nicholson, pp. 50–78.

Woolf, Leonard. 1921. "Pearls and Swine". In *Stories of the East*. Richmond: Hogarth Press, pp. 21–44.

TWO

COMPANIONABLE THINKING

STANLEY CAVELL

It was while I was thinking about preparing a text in which I would attempt to take further some earlier thoughts of mine concerning Wittgenstein's reflections on the concept of "seeing something as something", what he calls seeing aspects, which dominate Part II of *Philosophical Investigations*, that I reread the paper (I

This essay was written for and appears in *Wittgenstein and the Moral Life: Essays in Honor of Cora Diamond*, edited by Alice Crary, published by MIT Press in 2007. A version was given as the Hetman lecture at Columbia University in 2006. The "further thoughts" concerning Wittgenstein's reflections on "seeing as" occur in my paper "The Touch of Words," written for a vol-· ume edited by William Day and Victor J. Krebs for Cambridge University Press, scheduled to appear in 2008.

first encountered it as a lecture) that Cora Diamond—a philosopher whose work I have for years been particularly and continuously grateful for—entitles "The Difficulty of Reality and the Difficulty of Philosophy", a piece in which at a certain point she deploys an idea of mine in a way I found heartening and distinctly instructive. Eventually, I found that the rereading of her paper had made so strong an impression upon me that I came to feel compelled to articulate a response to it, however unsure I felt my philosophical ground might prove to be. Diamond's paper takes up certain extremities of conflict associated with phenomena of what she calls the difficulty of reality (call this a difficulty of change, a difficulty that philosophy must incorporate), cases in which our human capacities to respond—she in effect says the bases or limits of our human nature—are, for some, put to the test, threatening to freeze or to overwhelm understanding and imagination, while at the same time, for others, the phenomenon, or fact, fails to raise, or perhaps it succeeds only in raising, an eyebrow. Examples range from instances of being struck dumb by sublime beauty, to speechlessness before horror.) The principal matter Diamond treats in her paper is the fact, and the understanding of the fact, of our entwinement with the non-human world of animals, specifically and most extendedly our relation or relations to the mass preparation of animals as food for humans. It is a matter to whose implications

I have hitherto not devoted consecutive thought—a matter I now feel I have avoided.

I say at once that while relations to animals have come up variously, if intermittently, in my writing over the years, I am neither practiced in the theory of animal rights nor committed in my daily life to vegetarianism. But an idea which is said to test or threaten the limits of human nature reminds me that in my early reflections on Wittgenstein's study of seeing something as something I raised the issue <u>whether it makes sense to speak of seeing others or ourselves *as* human</u> (as opposed to what?). If it does then it makes sense to suppose that we may *fail* to see ourselves and others so—a purported condition I went on to call "soul-blindness". ✓ A subtext of my reflections to follow here is <u>the question whether there is a comparable blindness we may suffer with respect to non-human animals.</u>

The obvious bearing of Wittgenstein's study of seeing something as something on Diamond's wish to have us ponder the human and the intellectual challenges of the mass production of animals for food, lies in its suggestion that the extreme variation in human responses to this fact of civilized existence is not a function of any difference in our access to information; no one knows, or can literally see, essentially anything here that the others fail to know or can see. But then if one concludes that the variation is a function of a response to or of an attitude toward information that is shared, one may suppose the issue is of some familiar form of moral disagreement. Diamond's discussion specifically questions this supposition. One peculiarity of the case of breeding animals for the manufacturing of food, beyond the extremity of responses ranging from horror to indifference, unlike difficulties over the death penalty, or the legitimacy of a war, or the torture of prisoners, or euthanasia, or abortion, is that the issue is one that touches the immediate and perhaps invisible choices of most of the members of a society every day. Further, those who are indifferent to or tolerant of the mass killing of animals for food may well regard the purpose of the institution as producing an enhancement of modes of human life's greatest pleasures, from the common pleasures of sharing nourishment to the rare pleasures of consuming exquisite delicacies. It seems safe to say that no one of balanced mind thinks it an enhancement of human pleasures to perform executions or abortions or to torture. (Nietzsche may have exceptionally divined pleasure taken in such activities, and Himmler may have shared his view in warning the minions under his command that their deeds of extermination must be carried out soberly and dutifully.) The variation of attitudes that Diamond's discussion stresses between the horror of individuals and the indifference of most of society considers moments in which the variation of response seems one between visions of the world, between how its practices are regarded, or seen, or taken to heart, or not.

Wittgenstein's reflections on seeing aspects (most memorably using the Gestalt figure of a duck-rabbit to demonstrate incompatible ways of reading or seeing a situation) was brought into more general intellectual circulation when Thomas Kuhn used the idea of a "Gestalt switch" specifically in understanding certain crises in intellectual history, particularly in the history of science. But in Wittgenstein's elaboration of his reflections on the phenomenon he emphasizes that "hugely many interrelated phenomena and possible concepts" (p. 199) are brought into play, among them the concept of merely knowing (p. 202), and of reading a poem or narrative with feeling and merely skimming the lines for information (p. 214), and of being struck by, or blind to, a likeness, and of a picture as helping one to read with the correct expression (*ibid.*). I might characterize Diamond as raising the question of what I will call inordinate knowledge, knowledge whose importunateness can seem excessive in its expression, in contrast to mere or unobtrusive or intellectualized or indifferent or stored knowledge, as though for some the concept of eating animals has no particular *interest* (arguably another direction of questionable—here defective—expression). I think of a remark of Freud's in rehearsing the progress of coming into one's own through the talking cure: "There is knowing, and there is knowing."

And I suppose, in another register, this variability of condition is what Paul, in his first letter to the Corinthians, cites in the phrase "now I know in part".

I think too of my efforts to understand the appeal to the ordinary in the philosophical practices of the later Wittgenstein and of J. L. Austin, hence of the tendency they counter in Western philosophy, since at least Plato's Cave, of seeking systematically to transcend or to impugn the ordinary in human existence. The vivid extremes in responding to the world-wide existence of food factories is a cautionary, even lurid, example warning against supposing that the ordinary in human life is a *given*, as it were a *place*. I would say rather that it is a task, as the self is. I sometimes speak of the task as discovering the extraordinary in what we call ordinary and discovering the ordinary in what we call extraordinary; sometimes as detecting significance in the insignificant, sometimes as detecting insignificance in the significant. These are reasonable abstracts of what I recurrently find to be tasks of philosophy. And the sense of one familiar replacing a contrasting familiar is what I mark in the title of an earlier text of mine as "The Uncanniness of the Ordinary".

I will not arrive here at some conclusion about how far the concept of seeing aspects may bear on either inordinate or insipid expression. Such a suggestion comes up inconclusively a couple of times in what follows. Its point is to specify moments at which we know we stand in need of a convincing account of the ex-treme differences of response to the eating, and other questionable uses, of non-human animals—whether or when we count this as ordinary or as extreme—since in lacking it we betray a register of our ignorance of ourselves.

In the paper of Diamond's that I begin from here her reflections are principally cast as a commentary on moments from the presentation depicted in a pair of stories by J. M. Coetzee with the title "The Lives of Animals". The pair appear under this title as two of the seven chapters that make up Coetzee's novel *Elizabeth Costello*. The pair also appear in a separate volume also entitled *The Lives of Animals*, this time accompanied by responses from five writers from various disciplines. It is this latter volume that Diamond considers. She stresses her finding herself, in one decisively conse-quential respect, in a different, isolated, position from each and all of these five respondents, despite the fact that she and they all express unhappiness with the state, and the understanding of the state, of the human rela-tion to the non-human animal world. We shall come to Diamond's isolating difference in due course. I trust that I shall not refer to subtleties in either Coetzee's or Diamond's texts without quoting passages from them sufficient for judging them.

The first of the pair of Coetzee's stories features a lecture to a college audience in the United States given by a fictional Australian writer named Elizabeth Costello as part of the two or three day celebration in which she is being honored by the college. In the opening moments of her lecture Costello reports herself unable to put aside her perception, or vision, in all its offensiveness, that in the treatment of animals in what she calls our food factories we are, to "say it openly . . . surrounded by an enterprise of degradation, cruelty and killing which rivals anything that the Third Reich was capable of, indeed dwarfs it, in that ours is an enterprise without end . . ." (p. 65).

In the second of the stories Diamond is responding to, Coetzee includes near its beginning a letter from someone that Elizabeth Costello's son, who teaches at the college, describes as a poet who has been around the college forever. I quote most of the words of the poet's letter, anticipating my wanting to return to various of them:

"Dear Mrs. Costello, Excuse me for not attending last night's dinner. I have read your books and know you are a serious person, so I do you the credit of taking what you said in your lecture seriously. At the kernel of your lecture, it seemed to me, was the question of breaking bread. If we refuse to break bread with the executioners of Auschwitz, can we continue to break bread with the slaughterers of animals? You took over for your own purposes the familiar comparison between the murdered Jews of Europe and slaughtered cattle. You misunderstand the nature of likenesses . . . to the point of blasphemy. Man is made in the likeness of God but God does not have the likeness of man. If Jews were treated like cattle, it does not follow that cattle are treated like Jews. The inversion insults the memory of the dead. It also trades on the horrors of the camps in a cheap way. . . . Forgive me if I am forthright. You said you were old enough not to have time to waste on nice- ties, and I am an old man too. Yours sincerely, Abra- ham Stern."

Costello's daughter-in-law, with whom she does not get along, refers to the letter as a "protest", and the let- ter does seem to collect, as if to preempt, a number of attacks a reader might want to launch against Costello's speech. But, especially in light of the daughter-in-law's general dismissal of Costello's sensibility (and without speculating about what may be causing it), we can be sure that this is not enough to say about the letter's an- guish. In particular the letter avoids considering the specific understanding Stern expresses to account for his absence at last night's dinner. Along with other omissions among the appeals Stern addresses to logic in his distress—to matters of what follows from what— while Stern opens with the coup of raising the ques- tion of breaking bread in this context of an invitation to dinner, he omits to say why he had refused precisely to break bread last night with Mrs. Costello. Was this because her words have reached to the point of blasphemy, to dishonoring the work of God? (It is an issue for certain thinking about the Holocaust whether it should be represented at all.) Or was it because she insults the memory of the dead? Or because she invokes horror cheaply? Oddly, or ironically, these are causes Costello could well find pertinent to her own sense of horror, or as she sometimes puts it, disorientation. But this is not how Stern introduced the idea of breaking bread. He was granting (I assume) the truth of the idea that we (are right to) refuse to break bread with the executioners at Auschwitz. That black meal would, let us say, curse communion, incorporating—symbolically, it goes without saying, surely—the human ingestion of bread as the body and wine as the blood of divinity.

Stern's refusal of communion with the executioners at Auschwitz forms a sort of major premise, as it were, of the syllogism he attributes to Costello. Her minor premise is that the slaughterers of animals are in a moral or spiritual class with the executioners at Auschwitz. From which the conclusion follows that we (are right to) refuse to break bread with these further slaughterers. But are we to take it that Stern finds Costello's offensive fault of argumentative assimilation to warrant assimilating her to (receiving a treatment of shunning precisely marking the treatment warranted by) the executioners of Auschwitz, beyond the pale of shared bread? This reaction would seem to make his perception of Costello's fault quite as inordinate as he takes her perception of the slaughterers of animals to be. And/or should this count as Stern's doing what he promised at the outset of his letter to do, namely taking what Elizabeth said in her lecture seriously?

Taking expressions seriously, or a sense of difficulty with realizing this project, is a way I might characterize what Diamond names "the difficulty of philosophy", something she understands to inhabit or to be inhabited by "the difficulty of reality". I associate this mutual existence with what I have sometimes discussed as a chronic difficulty in expressing oneself, especially in its manifestation as finding a difficulty or disappointment with meaning, or say with language, or with human expression, as such. It is a disappointment I find fundamental to my reading of Wittgenstein's *Philosophical Investigations*.

In an essay from 1978, which she entitles "Eating Meat and Eating People", Cora Diamond identifies herself as a vegetarian and specifies her motive in writing about the question "How might I go about showing someone that he had reason not to eat animals?" as that of attacking the arguments and not the perceptions of philosophers who express the sense of "the awful and unshakable callousness and unrelentingness with which we most often confront the non-human world".

The arguments, familiarly in terms of animal rights, she finds not just too weak, but the impulse to argument at this level to be itself morally suspicious. I have I think felt this way when, in response to my expressing doubt that there are moral truths for whose certainty moral theory should undertake to provide proofs, philosophers more than once have proposed "It is wrong to torture children" as a certain truth to which moral theory has the responsibility of providing an argument, and at least one philosopher added: an argument strong enough to convince Hitler. In *The Claim of Reason* I reply to this train of thought by saying that morality is not meant to check the conduct of monsters.

I have not, I believe, anywhere considered in detail the dangers of allowing oneself to judge another to exhibit monstrousness. Perhaps this has been because I felt sure that I would be told that the danger of such a judgment is that others might take it into their heads to judge me to be a monster, without argument. It does not, I have to say, make me feel safer to suppose that my defense against a judgment of my monstrousness must be to discover an argument to combat it. The danger I still feel worth pursuing is that, or how, I might discover monstrousness in myself. What is Thoreau seeing when he declares, "I never knew a worse man than myself"?

I do not imagine that it has been a sense of poor argumentation on behalf of vegetarianism that has thwarted my becoming vegetarian. A clear inkling of the pertinence of the choice of that form of life for me was likely, I have thought, to present itself in consequence of my discovery of my love of Thoreau's multiple intelligence. I recall the a strong effect upon me of his saying that he has no objection to young boys learning to hunt and to fish—taking him to mean that in the age of innocence (the period Emerson calls the "neutrality" of boys) the young should feel in themselves that they are part of, equal to, the wildness of nature, that they sense and relish, not fear, or distrust, their own, let's say, animal aliveness—and his going on to cite the day on which, as Thoreau reports it, he discovered that in fishing he felt a certain lowering of respect for himself. It is from about then, backed by further of his observations, that I have sometimes half expected an analogous feeling to come my way. (Despite the fact that there was no one in my early life from whom to learn how to hunt and to fish.)

In Diamond's earlier essay, she isolates a line from a poem of Walter de la Mare's—"If you would happy company win" (namely the companionship of "a nimble titmouse")—and says of it (in contrast to the idea shared by the five commentators accompanying Coetzee's stories) that it presents "a different notion [of a non-human animal, namely], that of a living creature, or fellow creature which is *not* a biological concept", p. 328). What she explains she means by her different notion is one that is not the concept of an animal possessing this or that interest or capacity in common or at variance with our human interests or capacities, but one that "means a being . . . which may be sought as *company* [Diamond's emphasis]." It is the experience of company, say of proving to us that we are not alone in the world, and not an argument about the animal's biological powers, that on Diamond's view places consuming the animal out of reasonable bounds.

I recall passages in various texts of mine in which I have over the years been prompted to record, coming it could seem from nowhere, encounters with animals, real and imaginary. Thinking of Emerson at the moment (perhaps it was Thoreau) observing a squirrel arching across a field and his being prompted to say that squirrels were not made to live unseen, I am moved to record, from a time within the childhood of my two sons, my watching almost every day during the early weeks of winter the following scene play itself out beyond the kitchen window looking into the back garden of our house. We had strung a thin rope diagonally across a corner angle of the garden fence in order to suspend from the middle of the rope a bird feeder. This was designed to keep the two or three most familiar neighborhood squirrels away from the seeds before the birds had a chance at them. When initially the squirrels tried to maneuver themselves along the rope, something about it (its thinness, or its slack) foiled them.

Then the next day one of the squirrels negotiated the rope all the way to the feeder and tipped it so that some of its seeds fell to the ground, thus providing a repast for his (or her) companions and, eventually, himself or herself. I was surprised at how quickly it became obvious to me that on successive mornings it was invariably the same genius performing this mission on behalf of this little group. Before our family devised a further way to protect the birds' interests, I inwardly looked forward each day to encountering and saluting this gesture of virtuosity and careless sociability. Since it was in part my seeds that this benefactor distributed and ate, it expresses my sense of the situation to say that, as I observed him while having my morning coffee and roll, I was breaking bread with him, in common if not reciprocally.

What would follow? This sense is, I agree, perfectly incompatible with the idea of eating the fellow. But I have in any case never had such an idea with respect to squirrels. The idea has in the past been proposed to me with respect to rabbit and to horse and to snails. In each case I, as it were for the sake of philosophy, tried each just once. But my inward cringe at the idea of repetition in these cases did not transfer to my other carnivorous habits.

Nor am I tempted here to a hard conclusion about my inconsistency, although I am impressed, as Diamond is, by Costello's rueful admission, along with her inordinate knowledge of the use of animals for food, on her relative complaisance, anyway willingness, in wearing leather shoes and carrying a leather purse. (I suppose the admission is to ward off the attribution to herself of an unknowable purity of spirit.) Diamond speaks in this connection of inescapable but "bitter compromise". This greatly interests me and I mean to return to it.

 Diamond's emphasis on "company"—earning the companionship of the titmouse—is a fairly exact pre-cursor, etymologically, of Coetzee's Abraham Stern's sense in his letter of "breaking bread", an idea that Stern charges Costello with pressing into cheap service but which Diamond takes from Costello with utmost seriousness. This means that she takes seriously the inordinateness in Costello's response, I mean brings into question just what is disproportionate about it. (One could say she respects Costello's brush with mad-ness.) And perhaps she therewith brings into question whether proportionateness is the question. Here is a place we might ask whether it would be helpful to think of Costello to be seeing animals *as* company. But rather than intensifying insipid knowledge, this appeal to seeing something as something seems here to etio-late inordinate knowledge, or rather to make the com-pany of animals something less than a fact, namely the fact that they *are* (not serve as) company (for some, sometimes). Diamond emphasizes Costello's state of raw nerves or, as Costello sometimes describes it, her insecurity with her own humanity.

Diamond gets quickly in her Coetzee essay to that moment she takes most signally to differentiate her perception of his tale, hence to isolate herself, from the position of those who had been invited to respond to it. She focuses on the moment—one she discovers essentially to be passed by in their responses—in which Costello declares herself to be, analogously with Kafka's great ape in Kafka's tale "Address to an Academy", [quoting Costello] "not a philosopher of mind but an animal exhibiting, yet not exhibiting, to a gathering of scholars, a wound, which I cover up under my clothes but touch on in every word I speak" (p. 71). In thus taking her own existence to be one among the lives of animals in the story, it becomes the chief subject, or object, of the story, the singular life depicted in it that counts as multiple, the human as the animal of multiple lives, say drawn between wild and tame, or this way with one person those ways with others, open and hidden, old without being sure how to be old, capable of indecorousness in her work, suffering in, and suffering from, what she says, from her own indictment by it. Since Diamond rejects, congenially to my way of seeing things, the idea of *a* way, or a *set* of ways, for all to see, in which non-human animals differ from human animals, a way that explains why we might not wish, or allow ourselves, to eat them, I take the suggestion to be that the realms differ, and hence are akin, endlessly, as in the case of the separation, or differences, between the human and the divine. (The appearance of the religious in Coetzee's tale repeatedly becomes pressing. This must be mostly for another time.) For example, an animal's way of eating—and so the diet integral to an animal species' life form—differs from human eating as significantly as an animal's mating or parenting or building or foraging or bonding or mortality or attention or expectation or locomotion differs from, and is analogous to, one might sometimes say is an allegory of, their forms in human life.

Coetzee's book opens this way: "There is first of all the problem of the opening, namely, how to get us from where we are, which is, as yet, nowhere, to the far bank. It is a simple bridging problem, a problem of knocking together a bridge. People solve such problems every day. They solve them, and having solved them push on."

(In my piece on the aesthetics, or writing, of the *Investigations*, I am surprised to recall that I speak of a near and a far shore and of "the river of philosophy that runs between". The near shore is the perspective of philosophical "problems", listed by Wittgenstein in his Preface as "the concepts of meaning, of understanding, of a proposition, of logic, . . . and other things." The far shore is the further perspective I describe, or standpoint, "from which to see the methods of the *In-*

vestigations, their leading words home, undoing the charms of metaphysics, a perspective apart from which there is no pressing issue of spiritual fervor, whether felt as religious, moral, or aesthetic". And I go on to say: "One [shore] without the other loses the pivot of the ordinary, the pressure of everyday life; one without the other thus loses, to my way of thinking, the signature of the *Investigations*. There remains a question of priority. From each shore the other is almost ignorable, and each imagines itself to own the *seriousness* of the *Investigations*' work." (*The Cavell Reader*, pp. 382–383.) I should confess that I like to understand Cora Diamond's title for her already classic collection *The Realistic Spirit* as encoding these banks or shores, indicating that philosophy is perpetually a matter of tracing the loss and recovery (revised, reviewed) of the ordinary, of subjecting to criticism what we would like in philosophy to insist upon as necessarily real—specifically to criticism out of the spirit of realism, of how the human animal actually, let us say, forms its life and its understanding of its life.)

I take Coetzee's repetition, in his book's opening that I just now quoted, of "solve" or "solving", three times in two adjacent sentences, ironically but tenderly to picture "people", in attempting to make human life a series of problems, as attempting to construe their existence as itself a problem, an intellectual puzzle to solve and from which to push on. Nietzsche enters a similar complaint of intellectualization against our species, in its regarding life "as a riddle, a problem of knowledge", in *The Genealogy of Morals*. (I cannot but think that Cora Diamond was as intrigued as I to see Coetzee's opening chapter given the title "Realism".) *Philosophical Investigations* is in effect a portrait of the unsatisfiability of the human species with its solutions, a portrait—hardly the first—detailing human life as one of restlessness, exposure, insecurity; and more specifically, of what in an essay of mine on its aesthetics I identify as its articulation of the modern subject, namely its expected reader, as someone characterized by, among other traits, perversity, sickness, self-destructiveness, suffocation, lostness, strangeness, etc.

This may helpfully return us to the question of taking seriously Elizabeth Costello's notation of herself as an animal wounded, but with a wound (unlike other suffering animals) that she exhibits and does not exhibit. That she specifies her concealing it under her clothes immediately alerts us to the most obvious, or banal, unlikeness between her condition and that of other animals, namely just that her species wears clothes. And since what is concealed, and not concealed, under her clothes, we are allowed to assume—are we not?—is an aging but otherwise unharmed woman's body, the torment she expresses is somehow to be identified with the very possession of a human body, which is to say, with being human. (I say "otherwise unharmed". I am assuming that there is no visible remnant of harm from the event she describes in a later chapter when, half a century ago, she allowed herself to be picked up by a tough who beat her up when she found she wanted to repel his advances. She suffered a broken jaw and she describes its treatment and its healing. What counts as a wound persisting from that incident is her perception that the tough took evident pleasure in beating her; this produced in her what she describes as her first knowledge of evil, something not hidden by clothes. I do not know Coetzee's attitude toward the work of Freud, let alone Lacan. but I cannot put aside a suggestion I take that there is something specifically wounded in the normal female body.)

I emphasize two peculiarities about this revelation of the woundedness that marks being human. First, since the stigmata of the suffering are coincident with the possession of a human body, the right to enter such a claim universally to other such possessors, has roughly the logic of a voice in the wilderness, crying out news that may be known (inordinately) to virtually none, but to all virtually. It is a voice invoking a religious, not alone a philosophical, register: it is uninvited, it goes beyond an appeal to experiences we can assume all humans share, or recognize, and it is meant to instill belief and a commentary and community based on belief, yielding a very particular form of passionate utterance, call it prophecy. We could say that the object of the revelation is not simply to touch but to announce the wound that has elicited its expression and that gives it authority: Costello had said, in matching our behavior with that in the Third Reich: "*Ours* [our mass manufacturing of corpses] is an enterprise without end." It is an inherently indecorous comparison, not to say offensive, and perhaps deliberately a little mad; fervent news from nowhere. The right to voice it is not alone an arrogation of a claim every human is in a position to make, the sort of claim philosophy requires of itself, in speaking for all; it is also a judgment that distances itself from the human as it stands, that finds human company itself touched with noxiousness. (As if the mass slaughter of animals in effect negates or disenchants the concept, the possibility, of sacrifice.)

Here is a place at least to mention the apparent congruence between Costello's comparison of food factories and concentration camps with a pair of sentences attributed to Heidegger in an interview (by Philippe Lacoue-Labarthe, quoted by Maurice Blanchot), translated and printed in an issue of *Critical Inquiry* a few years ago devoted to Heidegger and Nazism. Heidegger is reported to have said: "Agriculture is now a mechanized food industry. [This much appears essentially word for word in Heidegger's well-studied text "The Question Concerning Technology" from 1955. The attributed pair of Heidegger's sentences continues:] As for its essence [that is, technology's essence] it is the same thing as the manufacture of corpses in the gas chambers and the death camps, the same thing as the blockades and the reduction of countries to famine [a reference, I assume, to Stalin's starvation of four million Ukrainian kulaks in the early 1930's], the same thing as the manufacture of hydrogen bombs." I rather imagine (but this is not essential to my reflections) that Coetzee knew this citation linking the food industry with, among other things, the death camps and that he meant to be putting Heidegger's words to the test in his novel, in effect to ask whether such a view is credible coming anywhere but from an old artist, tired of and sickened almost to death by the responses she receives late in her life of words, crazed by their reality to her together with their loss of interest to others and jarred or compelled by her imagination into welcoming the offense she may cause. One of the moments in Heidegger's *What Is Called Thinking?* that I have been most impressed by is his description of Nietzsche, in trying to reach his contemporaries with his perception of the event of our murder of God. Heidegger writes: "most quiet and shiest of men, . . . [Nietzsche] endured the agony of having to scream." I find it illuminating to think of Elizabeth Costello, in her exhausted way, as screaming.

A further detail suggesting the presence of Heidegger's *What Is Called Thinking?* in Coetzee's text lies in that opening picture of a reader's journey, or a life's journey, as from a near to a far bank, posing a problem from which "people" are able to "push on"; Coetzee calls it, speaking for these problem-solvers, a "bridging problem". Heidegger says early in this book of his, with respect to the passage from our scientific or intellectualized mentality to authentic philosophical thinking, that "There is no bridge here . . . only the leap." It follows that the opening paragraph of Coetzee's novel describes us, human beings pushing on, getting on, going along, solving problems (in terms, I take it, dictated by others) as not in a position, or a place, for thinking, or for what is to be called thinking.

One in whose imagination Heidegger survives as a serious thinker is apt to have had to find a way beyond the sense that his thought comes to direct itself as an apology for the practices of Nazism (despite certain of his "reservations" concerning its theories). And, since it is Elizabeth Costello's comparison of food factories with death camps that invoked Heidegger's linking of the camps with the agricultural industry, I mark her difference from Heidegger at the point at which Cora Diamond (in contrast to the initial silence on the point by the five commentators published together with Coetzee's pair of stories), unveils (as it were) her now inescapable knowledge of her hidden yet unconcealed wound. Heidegger acknowledges no such wound for him to confess (for *him*), nor any pain out of which to scream, and it is perhaps in this continence, or absence, that he is cursed.

I said that there are two peculiarities in Elizabeth Costello's invocation of human existence as wounded. The first is what I described as her identification of woundedness—judging from her own—with the condition of human embodiment, the very possession of the human body, as stigma. The second peculiarity is her claim that the evidence for her invisible/visible wound, or expression of it, is present, or, as she puts the matter, is "touched on", in every word she speaks. In my experience, a precedent for such a thought, or vision, is Emerson's way of speaking, epitomized in his declaration in "Self-Reliance", that "Every word they say chagrins us" (adding that "we know not where to set them right"). But what differentiates "them" from "us"? Every word Emerson hears chagrins him, and all the words he speaks are in essence, to begin with, the words of others, common bread. What other words are there? This means that every word he speaks is touched with, is fated to express, chagrin. To speak—the obvious signature expression of the human life form—is to be victimized by what there is to say, or to fail to say.

A topic that brings Emerson's chagrin to fever pitch is slavery. From "Fate": "Language must be raked, the secrets of the slaughter-houses and infamous holes that cannot front the day, must be ransacked, to tell what negro-slavery has been." Earlier in that essay Emerson had said: "You have just dined, and however scrupulously the slaughter-house is concealed in the graceful distance of miles, there is complicity, expensive races." This somewhat extends his earlier in the essay having spoken of "expensive races,—race living at the expense of race". I will not reargue here my sense that the repeated presence of the slaughter-house, together with the ambiguity of "race living at the expense of race"—meaning the human race living at the expense of animals but in this context unmistakenly meaning at the same time the white race living at the expense of the black—yields the perception, or vision, that slavery is a form of cannibalism. Essential to his "argument" is that the idea of language as having to be raked compresses a suggestion that in moments high and low the house of language is overrun, overcome, words must be searched for through wreckage and then with force and craft aligned into parallel, justified ranks on a page to work decorously together. Such matters—recalling what Diamond speaks of as the difficulty of reality and of philosophy—will have to be taken seriously if we consider whether it expresses the perception at issue to say that Emerson here sees slavery *as* cannibalism. This would make the concept of seeing-as a kind of explication of allegory, as when at the opening of *Walden*, Thoreau reports his vision of his townspeople of Concord, Massachusetts as observing practices meant to torment themselves, as though they are choosing, and not choosing, to make life a set of strange forms of penance, a vision that flares and fades; whereas I wanted to speak of the impression of cannibalism as perhaps irreversible.

I report also in this connection, as I have before, Thoreau's treating human feeding as such as a matter for anxious satire. In the account of his expenses, the literal listing of dollars and cents expended, for surviving his first year at Walden, Thoreau separately itemizes the cost of food, and he comments: "I thus unblushingly publish my guilt." Thoreau here perceives his very existence, the assertion of the will to live in the world by feeding himself, as without certain justification—there are debts in living, conditions of existence, uses to which he puts, or fails to put, the peaceable space cleared for him before he cleared it, that are uncountable. What makes them insupportable is the degree to which they are unnecessary. Then the quest in which an adventurous life may well be spent in search, or experiment, is to replace false by true necessaries, or means, to what one truly finds good (a philosophical quest as ancient as Plato's *Republic*), perhaps promising to allow the cloaking of the wound of existing to become superfluous.

Of course one may wish to ask whether Thoreau would not have more relevance to the way the world is if he were a little more realistic, say more open to compromise. (Albert Schweitzer in Africa, once a more formidable guide to existence than I suppose he is now, instead of (or in addition to) protecting his hoard from the ants, left little piles of sugar for them by his bed in his tent when he retired for the night. Is such a practice, from our contemporary perspective, anything more than precious or quaint? But perhaps it was not meant as more than one man's solace.) Yet Thoreau's key term "Economy", the title of the opening, longest chapter of *Walden*, precisely projects an unfolding register of terms in which compromise at its best—keeping accounts in a fallen world of one's interests and means and losses and wastes and returns and borrowings and dreams and terms (accounts of *all* of one's terms)—can best be articulated systematically and lived. Its moral could even be taken to be that of realism.

I predicted that I would want to return to the idea of compromise. Here more fully is Cora Diamond's response (in her Coetzee essay) when she takes up, in connection with my discussion in Part Four of *The Claim of Reason* of what I call our exposure to the other, Costello's reply to someone's suggestion that her vegetarianism comes out of moral conviction. Costello hesitantly deflects the suggestion, saying instead, "It comes out of a desire to save my soul." Diamond glosses this response as follows: "[We are not] *given* the presence or absence of moral community . . . with animals. But we are exposed—that is, we are thrown into finding something we can live with, and it may at best be a kind of bitter-tasting compromise. There is here only what we make of our exposure."

Can we specify more closely the cause and strength of the bitter taste of compromise, in a region in which taste may be thought to be everything? Taste—or some discrimination beyond what we readily think of as taste—seems at play in Costello's cautioning, or rebuking, her questioner (who had assured her that he has a great respect for vegetarianism as a way of life, thus in effect discounting her declaration of the threatened state of her soul beyond the matter of moral conviction) by saying: "I'm wearing leather shoes and carrying a leather purse. I wouldn't have overmuch respect if I were you." That is, there is still disproportion between what I know and how I feel and ways I behave, if less than there might be. Costello's questioner (he is identified as the president of the college honoring her) "murmurs": "Consistency is the hobgoblin of small minds. Surely one can draw a distinction between eating meat and wearing leather." "'Degrees of obscenity', she replies." Replies to *him*. (I merely take notice of this placement of Emerson's famous, and famously mocked, crack about the hobgoblin of consistency, slightly misquoted in the mouth of a decorous college president and used casuistically to take the sting from a declaration of one's soul threatened. Here is a welcome occasion to show Emerson's uncompromising words compromised; yesterday's radical words picked up by today's stuffed shirt.) But then what are we to make of Costello's use of "degrees"? She is implying her state as participating in obscenity, but the fact is that wearing leather, or the vision of preparation of it for human comfort and vanity, does not seem to cause her body dangerously to signal itself of its woundedness. Is it then in her case not the necessity of compromise that causes bitterness, but rather the discovery that she is, that her body is, capable of compromise? (This may suggest not a fastidiousness but a vanity of spirit.) But how does this reach to the sense of having to conceal, without concealing, a wounded body?

Is it a function of some perception of disproportion between saving one's soul and finding alternatives to wearing leather? This is in fact no easy matter to determine, especially if it begins to lead to questioning more globally the conditions under which our comforts generally are sustained and we undertake to examine work houses as closely as slaughter houses. As Emerson phrased the matter: however graceful the distance kept, "there is conspiracy, expensive races". I cannot doubt that Emerson is here (not for the only time) invoking Rousseau's perception of our stake in the social contract as that of conspirators, even recognizing that the perpetual failure of justice invites the threat of madness, of taking my participation in the difficult reality of my society's injustice or indifference or brutality as it were personally, a sense that seems to measure Elizabeth Costello's sense of isolation in her woundedness. The sense *happens*, happens even beyond sensibilities such as Hamlet's or Antigone's or Phédre's or Melisande's, unrelieved bearers of inordinate knowledge, of human exposure.

The direction out of Costello's condition (as it were against Kafka's report of a passage, or say bridge, to a higher species), barring withdrawal from the human race—that is, deciding to stay alive—is to sink within the race, or disguise herself as a voting member of it, at one with Hamlet in the perception that "Man delights not me; no, nor woman neither." Not prepared to resign from humanity, nor to display rage against others for failing to do so, which would uselessly increase the human being's suffering from itself ("horror of itself", Montaigne says, commending a more amiable wisdom), she insists upon her adorning and comforting herself with things of leather. I do not propose a competition between our degree of compromise with the subjection of animals to human demand and that of our compromise with the degree of injustice in our society. I remain too impressed with Freud's vision of the human animal's compromise with existence—the defense or the deflection of our ego in our knowledge of ourselves from what there is to know about ourselves—to suppose that a human life can get itself without residue into the clear. It is true that I have sometimes felt vegetarianism to be a way of declaring a questionable distance from the human animal, but that can hardly be the full reason for my not taking that path when it has beckoned.

I am in any case in accord with Cora Diamond's caution about what should count as a "reason" for or against eating meat. And I think I may have in the course of working through the present material to this point, learned something about the wish to declare distance from the identification with one's fellow human animals. I have in the past found that in moral confrontation I can never say in my defense (here disagreeing with a moment in the work of John Rawls), "I am above reproach", or found rather that to say so is to suggest that the other is morally less competent than I am. Now I find that, in response to reminders of the company we may keep with non-human animals, I cannot so much as say, "I am *not* above reproach". If the former defense falsifies my position by claiming an insupportable difference from others, the latter etiolates my position by claiming nothing in particular (declaring a generalized guilt in a guilty world), absolving myself from the task of responding to a reason for abstinence either by denying that I share the vision from which the reason derives its force (I do not see or treat all animals as companions), with or without urging a different vision (eating animals affirms my evolutionary stage as a carnivorous, or rather omnivorous, animal), or by marking a difference in my taste that shields it from the vision (I do not eat species that I perceive as companions). What I would like to say is simply, "I am human"—but to whom can this plea be directed?

Some concluding questions, as of notes to myself. Speaking of saving one's soul, how does one understand the characteristic of religions to impose dietary restrictions? Here are vast regions in which universal commands, unlike moral considerations, serve effectively and consistently to define a separate community, and do not depend upon changing one's individual sensibility with respect to other of God's creatures. It puzzled me, in some way offended me, when, during my preparation for my Bar Mitzvah, the rabbi cautioned a small group of us, in discussing the prohibition against eating pork, that we were not to claim that eating pork was in itself a bad practice, merely that it was not *our* practice, and followed this announcement with a little shudder of disgust and an enigmatic smile, which got a laugh from the small group. Both the smile and the laugh had a bad effect on me. Is absolute obedience to a mark of difference, merely *as* difference, a serious business or is it not? Embarrassed by, and not yet ready to repair, my ignorance of the general state of philosophical argument concerning vegetarianism, for example concerning whether religious dietary restrictions are expected to come into consideration, I took an occasion to ask a young friend studying theology whether the matter is current there. Without answering that, she pointed me back to the astonishing opening book of Daniel, in which Daniel, who "purposed in his heart that he would not defile himself with the portion of the king's meat", contrives to refuse Nebuchadnezzar's lavish hospitality, or say dictation, and instead to have substituted for himself and his little group of young captives a meatless regime, and after ten days "their countenances appeared fairer and fatter in flesh than all the children which did eat the portion of the king's meat." However, this story of God's favor, or this part of it, feeds my suspicion of vegetarianism as asserting a moral superiority to the rest of humanity, and now based not on an entire way of life but on the sheer fact of abstinence from meat. (I assume it is internal to the motivation for constructing a moral theory of animal rights to neutralize this danger.) But surely it is justified to declare a difference from such as Nebuchadnezzar? No doubt, but in our world this may require assigning to others the role of Nebuchadnezzar.

Is the threat of inconsistency in relation to other animals a cause of comparable anxiety, or "bitterness", with our inconsistency in our moral relations with other humans—thinking, as examples, of the long and terrible list of treacheries for which one asks forgiveness, or forbearance, every year on the Day of Atonement?: asking pardon for sins, for wrong-doings, specifying transgressions committed under duress or by choice, consciously or unconsciously, openly or secretly, in our thoughts or with our words or by the abuse of power, or by hardening our hearts or by speaking slander or by dishonesty in our work, and so on. Take, as I like to, Emerson's remark about the foolish consistency of minds (little or large) as meant to have us consider what we are made of that we may be, and need not be, foolish (an affliction non-humans are free from). What is human flesh that its appetites, even needs, express, and threaten, the human soul? If there is a threat of madness (persistent and silent outrage or despair are perhaps enough) in reaction to horrors that others seem indifferent to, is there not an equal threat in finding that one is oneself inconsistent in responding to these horrors? What is a proper response to learning, and maintaining the knowledge, of the existence of concentration camps, or of mass starvation, or of the hydrogen bomb? I confess my persistent feeling that a sense of shame at being human (at being stigmatized for having a human body) is more maddeningly directed to the human treatment of human animals than to its treatment of its non-human neighbors. I think I do not overlook the point that in relation to non-humans we can take meaningful personal measures whereas in the human case, if we are conscious of it, we readily sense

helplessness. What then? Shall we unblushingly publish our guilt in remaining sane in a mad world? I
assume philosophy is meant to help us here, say help
us to be philosophical. But it is up to us to ask, to go
first, to wonder.

THREE

COMMENT ON STANLEY CAVELL'S "COMPANIONABLE THINKING"

JOHN MCDOWELL

Early in "Companionable Thinking," Cavell asks himself whether Cora Diamond's purpose in considering J. M. Coetzee's character Elizabeth Costello might be helpfully framed in terms of Wittgenstein's discussion of seeing aspects. What makes the suggestion plausible, he says, is that "the extreme variation in human responses to this fact of civilized existence is not a function of any difference in our access to information; no one knows, or can literally see, essentially anything here that the others fail to know." Later he answers the question in the negative; he concludes that the idea of seeing something *as* something is not helpful here because if we frame Diamond's thinking in terms of aspect seeing, we do not give proper weight to the fact that for her other animals simply *are* our fellows, not things we can see as our fellows if we can achieve an aspect switch. Diamond does not say something analogous to "It can also be seen as a duck." But Cavell does not revoke the thought he expressed at the beginning, that all relevant knowledge is universally shared.

If Diamond's topic were how we should respond to the treatment of nonhuman animals in the production of food, Cavell's apparently offhand remark that no one knows anything others fail to know would surely be wrong in an obvious way. I think this is actually irrelevant to Diamond's point. (In a less obvious interpretation, the remark might still seem questionable about Diamond, more relevantly but less straightforwardly. I shall come to that.) But by letting it seem that his remark might be open to objection in the straightforward way I have in mind now, Cavell begins to obscure Diamond's purpose in invoking Coetzee's character. There is a twist to this, because the paper Cavell is responding to is a graceful approach to a central strand in Cavell's own thinking. Cavell's response does not do justice to the wonderful way Diamond has found to cast light on Cavellian themes.

If it were right to think Diamond is raising an issue that turns on how nonhuman animals are treated in the food industry, knowledge about that would surely be relevant. And it seems obvious that, contrary to what Cavell seems to say, such knowledge is unevenly distributed. Many people know nothing, or next to nothing, about how food (in general, not just meat) is produced. And even if we restrict attention to those who are open to concern about whether all is well in meat production, so that they try not to be ignorant about it, there is surely always room to learn more detail. It seems obvious that some know more than others. But as I said, I think this is irrelevant to Diamond's point.

Let me give a brief and necessarily oversimplified sketch of Diamond's attitude toward eating meat. First, consider eating human beings. Imagine a world in which dead human beings are rendered into unrecognizable foodstuffs and fed to the living with a lie about the source, as in Edward G. Robinson's last film, *Soylent Green*. If someone thought there was a topic for debate here, about whether this might be all right (I mean independently of the obvious problem about the lie), that would merely show that Diamond's use of the phrase "human being" does not express everything many of us mean by it. (What we mean by it now, that is; nothing ensures that we keep our concepts.) In a similar way, for Diamond it is not a matter for debate whether it might be all right to eat our fellow creatures. (Which ones? How should they be treated before being killed? And so on.) Those who make meat eating into a philosophical topic of the usual kind just reveal that they do not mean what Diamond means by "fellow creature." And it would be missing her point if one relocated the demand for argument as a request for a justification—at any rate a justification of the sort philosophers typically want—for the claim that nonhuman animals are our fellow creatures in a sense that has that power to exclude debate.

Cavell's remark that no one knows anything concerning meat eating that others do not know might now seem questionable in a deeper way. It is tempting to say that Diamond thinks she knows something many others do not know: that nonhuman animals are our fellow creatures in her sense. But perhaps Cavell's remark is not so offhand, after all, and perhaps it is closer to correct at this deeper level. It is not that Diamond thinks she has a piece of *information* others lack. That would make Diamond's thinking merely a special case of the kind of philosophical approach she rejects. How could one reject a challenge·to justify the claim that the supposed information is indeed that? And how could one avoid casting the supposed information as the basis for an argument that meat eating is wrong?

For Diamond, as I said, it is not a topic for philosophical argument, at least of the usual sort, whether meat eating might be all right. It should not seem to change the situation if we imagine animal husbandry being as it is depicted in a certain genre of children's stories, in which the relations between farmers and their animals are like the relations between people and domestic pets. Such stories necessarily leave unmentioned how the animals' lives end, and if one views animals as Diamond does, one would have to see sending them to be turned into food, however friendly one's previous relations with them were, as a betrayal. Factory farming is not like farming in the children's stories, and this amplifies the evil of meat eating. But it is not the essential thing, whereas if one does not share Diamond's vision of nonhuman animals, the cruelty of factory farming easily becomes the essential thing. It enters into arguments of an ordinarily philosophical kind, addressing the question *which* meat one should not eat and leaving it possibly all right to eat meat produced from animals that are treated well, as in the children's stories.

For a sort of parallel, consider this. (The sense in which it is a parallel needs care, and it is noteworthy that Coetzee's Costello does not give such questions the care they need.) Suppose someone said the project of eliminating Europe's Jews would have been a lesser evil if its victims had been treated with the utmost consideration and kindness in all respects apart from being deprived of life, which would of course have been done, in this fantasy, as humanely as possible. Such a judgment could be seriously advanced only in the somewhat crazy environment of academic philosophy. It distorts the way how things actually were matters. How things actually were amplifies the horror, somewhat as the cruelty of factory farming amplifies the evil of meat eating, as Diamond sees things. But if we suppose ethical argument might warrant judgments to the effect that it would have been better if the Final Solution had been put into practice in such and such a different way, we bring that horror into the domain of debate, where it does not belong.

For another case of what I mean by talking of amplification, let me mention another of Diamond's examples of the difficulty of reality. In Ted Hughes's poem "Six Young Men" the poet-speaker contemplates, in the 1950s, a photograph taken in 1914, in which six young men are vividly present to the viewer. They were all dead soon after the photograph was taken. The poem is about a kind of impossibility the poet finds in trying to combine that fact, in a single mental embrace, with the vibrant aliveness with which they are present in the photograph. Diamond does not remark on this, but the sense of dislocation the poet expresses, from his ordinary means of taking in reality, surely comes more easily because of the specific facts about the photograph. His frame of mind is colored by the thought that the deaths of *these* young men were pointless in a way that goes beyond the pointlessness of just any death. But this is another kind of amplifier. It would have been a harder poem to write, but the sense of dislocation could still have been voiced if the young men had died peacefully after long and fulfilling lives.

I have brought in the Hughes poem partly because I want to stress that Coetzee's Costello is only one of Diamond's examples. Another is a kind of experience of beauty, in which one seems to confront something beyond the reach of one's ordinary equipment for taking in what one finds in the world. And there are others, too. Cavell notes, of course, that Diamond's topic is something with multiple instances, not just the difficulty Costello finds in the reality she takes to be constituted by human treatment of nonhuman animals. But he talks as if Diamond's purpose in discussing Coetzee's work—which certainly occupies much of her attention in the paper he considers—were something on the lines of inducing meat eaters to reflect on their practice, or on the spirit in which they engage in it. I think that obscures the point of Diamond's paper. Costello figures, for Diamond, only as exemplifying, in a richly elaborated way, something that is also exemplified in Hughes's poem, and the specifics of what obsesses Costello are in a way irrelevant.

As I said at the beginning, it is Cavell's own thinking that is getting short-changed here. Let me try to explain.

Hughes's poem ends like this:

To regard this photograph might well dement,
Such contradictory permanent horrors here
Smile from the single exposure and shoulder out
One's own body from its instant and heat.

Here we have in germ the structure Diamond finds in Costello's response to human treatment of nonhuman animals.

The poet acknowledges that contemplating the reality his poem is about might well dement. The putative reality Costello contemplates does something close to dementing her. Her response is over the top, notably in the unqualified way she equates our treatment of nonhuman animals with the Holocaust.

The kind of difficulty both cases exemplify arises when something we encounter defeats our ordinary capacity to get our minds around reality, that is, our capacity to capture reality in language. That dislodges us from comfortably inhabiting our nature as speaking animals, animals who can make sense of things in the way the capacity to speak enables us. The special kind of animal life we lead comes into question. It is as if a beaver found dam building beyond its powers. In the poem the contradictory horrors "shoulder out / one's own body from its instant and heat." For Costello, it becomes a problem to live her particular case of the lives of animals: a life in which words are not just a distinguishing mark, as they are for human animals in general, but the central element. Her being as the animal she is, which is her bodily being, becomes a wound.

What Diamond aims to display by invoking Costello does not depend on whether what Costello responds to is the reality she takes it to be. Diamond, too, takes it to be a reality (though she manages not to be unhinged by it), but that is not the point. What Diamond reads Coetzee's depiction of Costello as conveying is something that, explicitly bypassing that question, I can put like this: if it is indeed a reality that most of us casually make a practice of eating our fellow creatures, with "fellow creatures" in that formulation of the putative reality bearing the sense it bears for Diamond and, presumably, Costello, then it is a reality such that to contemplate it head-on can shoulder out one's own body from its instant and heat, can dislodge one from comfortably living one's life as a speaking animal. One can appreciate that even if one does not suppose it is a reality; that is, even if one does not share that vision of nonhuman animals as fellow creatures.

Diamond's interest in Elizabeth Costello is as much in the commentators on Coetzee's Tanner Lectures as in the fiction itself. (Her topic is the Tanner Lectures, not the novel.) To varying extents, the commentators treat the fiction as a frame for presenting arguments—from which, as storyteller, Coetzee can distance himself—about the ethical standing of our treatment of nonhuman animals. This is an instance of what Diamond calls—following Cavell—"deflection." Coetzee's Costello responds, in a way that is not quite sane but is, in its way, appropriate, to a putative reality that dislodges her from being at home in her life as a speaking animal. The commentators substitute an issue that has only the different difficulty of academic philosophy. How convincing is such and such an argument? Does such and such a counterargument work? And so on.

Costello's vision of our dealings with other animals unhinges her. For Diamond, this is an analogue to a certain unhinged, though again in its way appropriate, response to another perception (or putative perception: here too, the point does not turn on its being, at least in any straightforward way, correct). The content of this other putative perception is that one is in a certain sense alone, profoundly unknowable by others. When one tries to get one's mind around this putative perception, one's ordinary linguistic repertoire fails one. That is what leads people to come out with forms of words like this: "Surely someone else cannot know it is *this* that I am feeling." Such wordings are a desperate attempt to force language to express a perception that is unhinging one in the way Diamond is interested in, threatening to dislodge one from one's life as a speaking animal.

In academic philosophy, this instance of the sense that one is losing one's ability to live the life that is natural for one gets deflected into an issue that has only the difficulty of ordinary philosophy: Do others have sufficient evidence for their judgments about one's inner life, or, symmetrically, does one have sufficient evidence for one's judgments about the inner lives of others?

Wittgenstein gives an extensive treatment of the wish expressed by saying "Someone else cannot know it is *this* that I am feeling," the wish to credit oneself with a language intelligible only to oneself. In standard readings, he is seen as addressing those academic questions about the strength of our grounds for judgments about one another. He is seen as uncovering, in the sense that skepticism is inescapable here, a merely intellectual error. Such readings are cases of deflection, like the commentators' responses to Coetzee's Tanner Lectures. They leave out what is really the whole point: that the impulse Wittgenstein treats originates in a case of being understandably unhinged by the sense that one's words are failing one, that one is losing the capacity to instantiate one's allotted life form as a speaking animal.

Academic treatments of skepticism about empirical knowledge in general can be seen in a similar light. They are a deflection from a response that is unhinged, though again in its way appropriate, to the perception, or putative perception, that in such supposed knowledge we are pervasively at the mercy of the world—a perception, say, of our finitude and dependence as empirical knowers.

That is a drastically abbreviated sketch of how Cavell explains the significance of philosophical skepticism. The role of Coetzee's Costello in Diamond's paper is not to raise the question whether Costello's unhinging perception is a perception of how things indeed are— that is, whether meat eating is what she thinks she sees it to be, which would certainly have implications about whether we meat eaters should continue with the practice. The role of Coetzee's Costello for Diamond is rather to provide an analogue for the unhinging perceptions of separation and finitude that, according to Cavell himself, constitute the real point of philosophical skepticism. And—just as importantly—the role of Coetzee's commentators for Diamond is to provide an analogue for how philosophy in the academic mode, in Cavell's own reading, avoids what is really at issue in its engagements with skepticism.

CONCLUSION

DEFLECTIONS

IAN HACKING

Cora Diamond's essay is deeply perturbing. It gives cause to think, to stop; that is, it gives cause not to speak while it is being taken in.

Elizabeth Costello began her first talk at Appleton College by saying,

> I want to find a way of speaking to fellow human beings that will be cool rather than heated, philosophical rather than polemical. . . . Such a language is available to me, I know. It is the language of Aristotle and Porphyry . . .
>
> (Coetzee, *The Lives of Animals*, 22)

Her list of proper names ends with Tom Regan.

It is a philosophical language in which we can discuss and debate what kinds of souls animals have, whether they reason . . . , whether they have rights in respect of us or whether we merely have duties in respect of them.

Costello does use that language during her first lecture, but it does not suffice. She needs another way to speak. That is one way to understand Diamond's title: there are difficulties of reality that are too stark for philosophical language. And that is a difficulty of philosophy.

Diamond's paper is far more than that too-simple gloss. Take note of the closing words: "how much that coming apart of thought and reality belongs to flesh and blood." I still have not properly taken that in.

The second half of Diamond's essay has important things to say about the very nature of Stanley Cavell's contributions to philosophy, as does he in response. Then John McDowell points out several ways in which to correct or improve Cavell's own reading of Diamond. He also graciously shows how some of her thoughts lead us back to some of Cavell's earlier philosophy. In these matters I am content to admire and shall not intervene.

PHILOSOPHICAL DIALOGUE

None of the three essays collected here is about animals. As McDowell reminds Cavell, Diamond uses Coetzee's

The Lives of Animals only as her *second* literary source for an example of difficulties. She does so to show us how the lecturer within the lecture, namely Elizabeth Costello, is "a wounded animal." She also (again, see McDowell) uses some of the intellectuals appointed to comment on the Tanner Lectures to show how they deflect Coetzee by imagining that he uses Costello as his mouthpiece for his own beliefs and practices.

Animals nevertheless set the tone of this book. Its puzzling title, *Philosophy and Animal Life*, reinforces that for the reader. Perhaps we think of animals, in reading Diamond, because she has, elsewhere, written more challenging philosophy about animals in English than anyone else in our times.[1] It also helps that Coetzee's philosophical dialogue does loom large in the background.[2] Indeed, that opening remark of Costello's could serve, as I have just said, as an introduction to one of Diamond's concerns.

Philosophical dialogue? Yes. Coetzee is a man of many genres. *The Lives of Animals* shows a mastery of the dialogue form greater than that of any philosopher in living memory. Calling his lectures a dialogue in the manner of Plato does suggest that there is a central speaker with a thesis to defend, that of the author. Simple minds may go on to infer that since Coetzee is a vegetarian, and so is the main speaker, Elizabeth Costello, therefore Costello is expressing Coetzee's argument for vegetarianism. So much the worse for simple minds. This is a philosophical dialogue composed by a great novelist. Diamond draws attention to its further implications *about* philosophical writing, in detail, in her footnotes 5 and 12.

Coetzee's two lectures form a dialogue in another sense, a dialogue of two parties, poetry and philosophy. That quarrel was launched in dialogue form by Plato himself. The first lecture is called "The Philosophers and the Animals"; the second, "The Poets and the Animals." Two primary poems in the second part are Ted Hughes's vivid portraits of the Jaguar (Coetzee, *The Lives of Animals*, 50–51). There it is before you, sheer animal life, immensely powerful, caged and mocked by mere people. This passage reinforces Costello's retort to Thomas Nagel in the first lecture: she knows what it is like to be a bat. First of all, it is to be full of life, bat-life, the joy of being a bat. In her much better words,

> To be a living bat is to be full of being. Bat-being in the first case, human-being in the second, maybe; but those are secondary considerations. To be full of being is to live as a body-soul. One name for the experience of full being is *joy*. (33)

Here I need to say a word about Cary Wolfe's introduction. Costello says, "For instants at a time, . . . I know what it is like to be a corpse" (32). Wolfe uses this line (without the "for instants") to commence a meditation on

Death and the Other. Indeed, he is taking up Diamond's own use of the sentence to remind us of human vulnerability. Yet Coetzee used it to introduce Life and Joy. Here is the argument: if we can, for a moment of complicated reflection, know what it is like to be a corpse, then we can the more easily know what it is like to be a bat. Again, Costello's own words: "Now I ask: if we are capable of thinking our own death, why on earth should we not be capable of thinking our way into the life of a bat?" (33). This is a nice instance of a philosophical argument being *tried out* in the course of a dialogue. Diamond shows us that Coetzee has written much more than a philosophical dialogue, but let us not thereby forget that he does use all of the dialogical tricks of the trade inaugurated by Plato.

Diamond cited poets in her essay, which was first used for a conference on literary language and only secondly for a conference in honor of Cavell. She also by implication entered the lists against Plato in the quarrel between philosophy and poetry. That is a nice uptake of the two distinct lectures delivered by Coetzee himself.

I would like to deflect the dismal tone of death that may emanate from some earlier parts of this book. Death is not interesting. Life is. Diamond fills us with foreboding, by starting with Hughes's poem. Coetzee and Costello used two of his other poems to fill us with pride of life, the joy of being, even when caged. Sure, we are caged, not by bars but by the nothingness on both sides of our time. But we don't have to pace around, conscious only of death caging life. Costello takes Hughes's poems to be a riff on Rilke's "The Panther." In the matter of death we need not accept what "the bars compel on the panther, a concentric lope that leaves the will stupefied, narcotized" (50).

REALITY, THE DIFFICULTY OF

Diamond used poets and novelists to make us experience some realities. Ted Hughes's poem makes us aware at one moment of six lads being so filled with life—and dead so soon after the snapshot. Czeslaw Milosz presents us with the inexplicableness of beauty, which is just there. Ruth Klüger brings us face to face with the incomprehensible goodness of another person.

And then there is Coetzee, who portrays Elizabeth Costello haunted by animal life distorted by breeding and killing. She is distraught by the reality of which she is so intensely aware. She is shattered by the meat industry, our callow inability to recognize and respect animal lives as lived, our creation of imbecile experiments on them, and our arrogant philosophies about them. She hates our incessant pointing at animals combined with our complete indifference to all but the pets. "Our" means "we adults," not children.

In each case, reality brings the poet or novelist up short, astonished, thunderstruck, whether by horror or by a sense of the sublime, and sensitive readers catch that by reading these works of art. It is the sheer *ther-eness* of the realities that Diamond experiences. Yet both Stanley Cavell and John McDowell evince, in very different ways, a caution about that. Cavell does so by wondering if we need to import some idea of seeing an aspect, of seeing *this* as the reality. McDowell does so by invoking putative reality.

SEEING AS

Cavell suggests that we start thinking about Diamond's essay in terms of "seeing an aspect," in part because what is needed, to come to share Costello's point of view about animals, is not more information but a different way of seeing things. We do, after all, know it all already, he suggests. McDowell rightly protests that a great deal of information about killing animals for human food is not generally known, and much of it might align one with Costello. In any event, the relations among see-ing, seeing aspects, and new information are subtle. I shall give three examples to illustrate Cavell's quotation from Wittgenstein, how "hugely many interrelated phe-nomena and possible concepts" are brought into play. Too many readers focus on duck-rabbits, which are pre-cisely not the point. Cavell mentions Thomas Kuhn as one such reader, the Kuhn of gestalt switches. We might call that the born-again version of seeing an aspect. Pascalian conversion (if I may so call it, only to make a contrast) is little by little, case by case, lived experience by lived experience.

Here is a vignette from Coetzee's *Boyhood*, published around the time that he was giving his Tanner Lectures of 1997 and 1998. He classifies the book as nonfiction. This is its second paragraph:

> At the bottom of the yard they put up a poultry-run and install three hens, which are supposed to lay eggs for them. But the hens do not flourish. Rainwater, unable to seep away in the clay, stands in pools in the yard. The poultry-run turns into an evil smelling morass. The hens develop gross swellings on their legs, like chicken elephant skin. Sickly and cross, they cease to lay. His mother consults her sister in Stellenbosch, who says they will return to laying only after their horny shells under their tongues have been cut out. So one after another his mother takes the hens between her knees, presses on their jowls till they open their beaks, and with the point of a paring-knife picks at their tongues. The hens shriek and struggle, their eyes bulging. He shudders and turns away. He thinks of his mother slapping stewing-steak down on the kitchen counter and cutting it into cubes; he thinks of her bloody fingers.[3]

No factory farming here, just three hens in a drab housing estate in the parched uplands of Cape Province.

The boy shudders and turns away. He sees what he sees, right there, but *he also sees what he did not see before*: the steak, bloody; his mother's fingers, bloody; the flesh and blood of something that was once alive, like the three chickens in the yard. He does not see it "as" blood. He sees it for what it is, blood. The experience stuck with Coetzee all his life. There is no new information, but his eyes are opened.

Next, take a simple fact about the meat industry that is not widely known. Commercially farmed turkeys in America are no longer biologically viable on their own. The tom has been bred to be so heavy that, aside from the fact that he can no longer walk but only totters, he cannot fertilize a female, for if he mounts her he will crush her to death. This may seem so gross, so demeaning of animal life, that, at the least, one refuses to participate in the turkey industry, declining turkey at festive occasions.

This looks like a clear example of McDowell's point. This is new information, not seeing an aspect of the American Thanksgiving festival. But not so quick. Does one have to experience this reality as gross, as demeaning, as insult not only to the birds but also to us who have created these sorry fowl? What if one sees only an efficient method of feeding low-fat protein to rich human beings hooked on meat? From the point of view of evolutionary biology, the species *turkey* (*M. gallopavo*) now flourishes in successful symbiosis with the species *man*, the latter providing the artificial insemination needed for part of the reproductive cycle. If that is how you see things, you may want to participate in the rituals of basting, carving, and eating that contribute to this evolutionary success story, which begins with Mesoamerican civilizations domesticating the bird.

Does it all depend on how you see things? Just possibly you can switch back and forth between the turkey as appalling and the turkey as evolutionary success story and so make this look like the classic seeing-as duck-rabbit. But that is not the way it goes. Cavell notes that both Costello and Diamond are horrified not only by what is done to animals but also by the widespread indifference of the humanity that eats them. He invites us to think of two different visions of the world. Quite so, but it also comes down to innumerable minutiae, whose effect may differ from attentive person to attentive person.

It is striking that English-language philosophizing about animals is (like so much else in analytic philosophy) usually about individuals. Points are made in terms of the suffering or death of an individual, even if they are killed en masse, in the herd. I have just pointed to the species. Cavell speaks of "breeding animals for the manufacturing of food." Breeding can mean rearing, propagating; it can also mean creating a new kind of animal. In the case of the turkey, we have bred a new kind of bird, our creation, just as stock-breeders have bred the Holstein and the Guernsey cow. Then these birds are bred (in the other sense of the word) by artificial insemination.

We now speed up the process of creating new breeds by genetic engineering. Oncomice are mice genetically altered so they will get cancer when young and so can be conveniently used in testing possible remedies. In all the debates about genetic engineering and animal rights, few worry about the monsters that we have brought into existence, millions of monstrous turkeys, tens of thousands of monstrous mice, deliberately made to get sick, suffer, and die. No one pickets Harvard University, which gets a royalty from each and every oncomouse until the patent runs out.[4]

Finally, take what was, for me, new information provided by Temple Grandin. She is not a philosopher but a person who rescued herself from autism by great courage and the sense that her anomalies make her better able than the rest of us to understand how animals think and feel. She has changed the practices of most American abattoirs and in so doing has made the animals' last walk down the alley of death less horrible. She helps them to go not only more gently into the night but also to meet their end in a way that is more dignified, for an animal.

She says she has done this by sharing their sensibilities. Autists and animals, she argues, think and experience in pictures, not words.[5] I am not so sure that an autistic sensibility was needed to do one of the important things she did. The fact is, however, that only an autistic person had the good sense to do it. She got down on her hands and knees and crawled along the final walkway, noticing what was scary as she passed. Her recommendations have been widely accepted: terrifying angles, shadows, bright lights, and sudden noises have been removed or subdued. There is money in it for the butchers, of course. Dignity be damned: a completely terrified animal on the death trip slows down production as badly as an epileptic attack on an old-time assembly line.

Grandin's measure of success, in making a slaughterhouse more "humane," is that *only one in four* of the victims becomes so frightened that it needs to be driven to its end with electric cattle prods. So here is the item of what was, for me, new information: *A slaughter house is judged to be humane if no more than a quarter of the animals have to be driven forward by electric shocks.* She states this in a matter-of-fact way: she is not an animal activist, only someone who, in this case, actively improves the deaths of animals. Her information was not highlighted—quite the opposite—but it caught my attention. It did not add much to my store of grisly facts about meat packing. But I experienced it strongly. We now need to torture only one beast in four before it is killed. In saying this, I in no way wish to minimize her achievement: it has done more to improve animal death than any philosopher ever will.

The word "torture" here is encouraged by our memories of the use of electricity in torturing men: electrodes to the testicles and so forth. But it seems to me that the information itself does the trick, if it has any effect. As a matter of fact, it appears to have no effect at all. Readers do not notice the information. Grandin's book was a runaway best-seller, on the *New York Times* list of the overall top ten for months. But I have never heard anyone mention the industry norm, that no more than a quarter of the animals on death row should be driven by electric prods.

To what extent should we acknowledge a moral component, to seeing matters differently or afresh? There is something wrong, morally lacking (I feel) with someone who does not shudder with the boy at Coetzee's vignette, who is not appalled at the way we have bred turkeys out of their turkeyness, who is not dismayed by the present standard for humane treatment of steers during their last few minutes.

PUTATIVE REALITY

McDowell resists "seeing as" as the correct analysis of such phenomena. To understand Costello's "difficulty of reality," we need not see things her way. We need not share her vision, her horror at the breeding, the producing, the killing, the packaging, and the eating. All we need to grasp is what Costello holds to be the reality. McDowell calls that putative reality. That suffices to explain her difficulty.

Costello, says McDowell, "is not quite sane" in her reaction to this putative reality. She is "unhinged" by it. That well expresses the reaction of Costello's daughter-in-law, Norma. Actually, when I read Coetzee's book, I never thought of Costello as other than sane. Wounded, yes. But unhinged? But let us proceed in the normal way, that is, Norma's way, treating her as a bit unhinged.

McDowell avoids a temptation that reeks of relativism, to say that the reality is horrific "for her" but need not be so "for us." The reality is horrific or it is not. Leave aside the question of which it is; what Costello takes to be reality *is* horrific. That is sufficient. We can understand why she reacts as she does to this putative reality, without quibbling about what is in fact the case.

I shall try to explain why "putative" may not help.

The trio of "putative reality," "unhinged," and "not quite sane" in the same paragraph creates a problem. To be unhinged is close to being deranged (one of the senses given by the *OED*) which is close to being mad. Some forms of madness are accompanied by a very weak grip on reality. Some mad people suffer from delusions. Those are part of *their* putative reality. A man, already with some minor manifestations of paranoid schizophrenia, increasingly becomes convinced that the minds (and hence the bodies) of his teenage children are being taken over by aliens, in the manner of *Invasion of the Body Snatchers*. (This is far from inconsistent with his experience, as many parents will agree.) He withdraws them from school, has them under constant surveillance, and moves his family to a cabin in the mountains so any aliens can be more readily spotted. His wife finally has to disappear with the children to preserve her and their sanity. So they have been abducted by aliens. This man's putative reality, if it were reality, would unhinge any father. But this man is not unhinged *by* his putative reality. These delusions, this putative reality, show *that* he is unhinged.

Does Costello's putative reality show that she is unhinged? Or is she unhinged by her putative reality?

Of course it is the second. For it to be clearly the second, it must be *reasonable* to suppose that the putative reality is what is the case, is the reality. But then Costello lives in a world, a reality, where her beliefs about what is going on are reasonable. If Costello does live in such a world (it's our world), then it is not putative reality but reality itself that unhinges her.

Perhaps we should speak not of the difficulty of reality but of the difficulty of experienced reality, of reality as experienced. This allows Elizabeth Costello her horror at the meat industry, the reality as she experiences it. It excludes the madman in his cabin because delusions are not reality as experienced, even if they are as painful to the deluded man as any experience he has ever had. I hope this is more faithful to Diamond's intentions than ether "putative" or "seeing as."

BARBED WIRE

Coetzee/Costello certainly managed to upset people by putting the comparison with the Holocaust up front.

McDowell has the most balanced description: Costello is "over the top." Cary Wolfe begins his introduction to the present book by invoking Lurie in Coetzee's *Disgrace*. The book ends with an extraordinary few pages in which Lurie puts to death a crippled dog with whom he has pieced together his own life (and the dog's too). Quite a number of dogs are to be killed. In case anybody should miss the point, Coetzee writes that Lurie and the vet "are engaged in one of their sessions of *Lösung*."[6] Yes, that is the German for the final solution.

Anyone who thinks Coetzee is simplistic in his use of the Holocaust comparison should read these pages. If you think Costello is upsetting, you ain't seen nothing yet. On the second to last page of the book, "He has learned by now, to concentrate all his attention on the animal they are killing, giving it what he no longer has difficulty in calling by its proper name: love" (*Disgrace*, 218).

That book is no more primarily about death than are the Tanner Lectures. They are more about dignity. A little earlier in the book Lurie cannot bear to leave the animals he has killed alongside hospital waste, road kill, and the filthy remains from a tannery. "He is not prepared to inflict such dishonor upon them" (144). He cannot stand seeing the dogs, stiff with rigor mortis, smashed by laborers a few days later so they will fit into an incinerator. So he takes the fresh corpses and burns them. "For the sake of the dogs? But the dogs are dead; and what do dogs know of honor and dishonor anyway? For himself then. For his idea of the world" (146). We are reminded of Costello, who says her not eating meat comes less out of moral conviction than from a desire to save her own soul (*The Lives of Animals*, 43).

Yes, to save the soul (a word that Costello uses fifteen times), but also out of a sense of respect for fellow creatures. Lurie "is convinced the dogs know their time has come. Despite the silence and the painlessness of the procedure . . . despite the airtight bags in which they tie the newborn corpses, the dogs in the yard smell what is going on inside. They flatten their ears, they drop their tails, as if they too felt the disgrace of dying" (*Disgrace*, 143).

Grandin doubtless senses the same knowledge in the animals in yards near abattoirs. The disgrace is not only in dying: one is horrified by the insult to animal life when turkeys are bred too big to walk or procreate; we have created a species that cannot have any dignity

In the three essays collected in this book, and in the introduction, death seems to be what matters in our treatment of animals, plus our indifference to the mass slaughter. Coetzee is more nuanced. Costello is just as appalled by Kohler's experiments on apes and by the sheer loss of dignity in using a tuxedo to dress up Kafka's Red Peter, the chimpanzee that matches Kohler's Sultan. One is reminded again of the "hugely many interrelated phenomena and concepts" that bear on the ideology of Costello, and, I dare to say it, of Coetzee.

To spin out the interrelations further, look at *Barbed Wire*, an astonishing book by Reviel Netz.[7] He tells how barbed wire was invented to keep cattle out of, or in, bits of the prairies, by inflicting sharp wounds on the dumb beasts. Thus was the Wild West won, and also the U.S. steel industry launched. On to the British invention of concentration camps in South Africa, on to 1914 and the Great War, which was less trench warfare than barbed-wire warfare. (One of Hughes's young men "lay calling in the wire, then this one, his best friend, / Went out to bring him in and was shot too.") On, of course, to the Holocaust and the gulags. Netz ends briefly with a muted scream about animals that is more ironic than Costello's, but just as impassioned.

1914 AND ALL THAT

Ted Hughes's poem "Six Young Men" had nothing much directly to do with animals or even the Holocaust, we all thought, until Netz reminded us of the strictly historical interrelations among the barbaric phenomena of cruelty.

I do not trust my own reactions to his poem. This is not a wholly personal matter; it bears on the question of information, what we know about reality, and how we experience it. There are several distinct points to make.

Among the difficult realities are the young men, their coming death, a stupid war, and the poem itself. McDowell points to the relevance of 1914: "the deaths of *these* young men were pointless in a way that goes beyond the pointlessness of just any death." (He, I, and doubtless the poet, share the judgment that the Great War was pointless stupidity; many people, including my own father, a loyal soldier in a later war, would not have agreed.)

What if the six had slammed their car into a tree after a drunken party? That would demand a wholly other poem; one can imagine several poems, each dislocating in a new way. McDowell himself continues in a more complex vein, saying that a different, harder poem to write would be about a photo of six young men who died after long and fulfilling lives. Would that really have the amplification, the sense of dislocation, of which he speaks so well?

What about a snapshot—no, a digital image taken on a cell phone—of four youngish Englishmen taken on 8 January 2005, their shoes shining, one bashful, one full of cocky pride—who were all four dead, exactly six months later, along with fifty-two other passengers whom they blew up on London Transport? In every case it is the rich embeddedness of the photograph that will mean something and that a great poet can turn into poems. It is not only knowledge that counts but a more general aura of meaning. The poem means most to a rather small class of readers, those to whom 1914 means something. The death of young men in pointless war is monstrous, but does the poem with all its allusions mean much to a citizen of one of the Koreas, close though she is to potential war?

McDowell notes that Cavell does not discuss the poem with which Diamond so powerfully begins her essay. There is a good reason for Cavell's abstinence. He is a grand master of American myths, and foreign ones carry no emotional weight for him. In British mythology of several generations, 1914 looms very large, even reaching, barely, to the present. It has nothing like that role in American self-identity.

To use the words of Elizabeth Costello, "This is a perspective you might expect from an ex-colonial" (*The Lives of Animals*, 57). She is Australian; I imagine that "ex-colonial" might not mean "former colonial" but something as precise as "from a country that is a former Euro-pean white colony and retains many marks of that." The year 1914, or rather 1915, is central to Australian mythology. ANZAC day, 25 April, is a national holiday, commemorating the Australian dead at Gallipoli, which happens to be *exactly* where and when Hughes' six young men died. It is important in Canadian mythology (mutatis mutandis, Vimy Ridge). There is an (absurd) movement afoot to give the last surviving Canadian soldier of the Great War a state funeral when he completes his allotted five score years and ten. Twenty-one guns, the Governor General, and lots of Mounties on horseback. Veterans of later wars still sell poppies on the streets on Armistice Day ("In Flanders Fields the poppies blow between the crosses row on row," penned by a Canadian medic at the battle of Ypres, May 1915). Americans who come up to give talks in Toronto in early November ask bemusedly, "Why are you wearing those cute little red flowers on your lapels?" I have perhaps said enough to suggest why I do not trust my reactions to the poem. McDowell is an ex-colonial; Coetzee, too. Diamond, of course, is not but studied in Oxbridge about the same time I did, and I can infer her exposure to the myths.

I found it salutary to stumble upon some of Ted Hughes's words about the poem. Speaking in New Zealand in 1976 he said:

> This is a meditation of a kind—on a photograph of six youths. And it's taken in a valley just below where I lived in Yorkshire and just before the outbreak of the First World War. These six youths were all friends of my father's. And the war came, and this photograph is just one among family photographs—so I've been hearing stories about these characters on this photograph for as long as I've been picking up the photograph and looking at it. . . . All these Yorkshire-men joined the Lancashire Fusiliers—they were all in the same company. They all trained together. They all went out together. They all fought together and so they tended to get killed together. So this was sort of the fairy-tale—my early stories—just a poem about these early anecdotes that I heard about these men.[8]

Later in the evening he read a three-part poem. "The first [part] I called, 'The Dream Time', and the last one is 'Remembrance Day', which is the November day when they sell poppies for the Armistice." He continued: "The poem is called 'Out', and the idea is to get rid of the entire body of preoccupation."

DEFLECTION

Hughes deflected his early obsession with his father's war. Coetzee did not deflect his boyhood horror of the hen-yard blood. I am using Diamond's word "deflect" here in a generous way. She took it from Cavell, who used it in a stunning metaphor about solipsism. Diamond said that initially, "I simply want the notion of deflection, for describing what happens when we are moved from the appreciation, or attempt at appreciation, of a difficulty of reality to a philosophical or moral problem apparently in the vicinity." Deflection in this sense substitutes a painless intellectual surrogate for real disturbance. Just as I deflect a blow by protecting myself with my forearm, or deflect justified anger by sincere humility, so (in Cavell's story) I deflect the reality of loneliness, of aloneness, or of unshared and unshareable mental or spiritual pain, by transposing it into the philosophical conundrum of skepticism about other minds, which has become an unemotional academic pursuit. We might call such deflection escapist.

Don't knock deflection. Deflecting is one of the things that we do quite well. Deflecting blows and deflecting anger is a good thing. Man is the Deflecting Animal. In daily Western life, women tend to be better at nonescapist deflection than men, who are dogged and dogmatic. In folklore, that is, in just-so stories about prehistory, it was early women who made the key deflections. They deflected fire from feared to friend. They deflected their families from foraging into planting, thereby setting our species on the road to planetary domination.

Deflection can be perfectly healthy, although we may prefer other words: Hughes worked out an obsession by writing certain poems, and then could cast it out.

On the other hand it is not for Coetzee to deflect his memory of the chickens or, a little later, of sheep. The boy goes to relatives who have a sheep farm because wool gets a good price in those days. He watches the weekly killing of a sheep for dinner, from the moment the workman picks out the one to die, "to the use of a harmless-looking little pocket knife" to extract "the great blue stomach full of grass, the intestines (from the bowel he squeezes out the last few droppings that the sheep did not have time to drop), the heart, the liver, the kidneys—all the things that a sheep has inside him and that he has inside him too" (*Boyhood*, 98–99). He also watches the castration of the lambs. Inside, the animal is just like me; outside, too, in the castration scene. When he has become a novelist, Coetzee does not deflect his boyhood shock by talking about the interests of the lambs being infringed, or the rights of the sheep being denied. Instead, he reinforces his feeling of the sheep as fellow creatures, so like himself, inside and out. He has no desire to cast this feeling out: later in life he delivers his Tanner Lectures.

ARGUMENT AS RHETORIC AND LOGIC AS FORENSICS

It is seldom obvious at first sight whether deflection is unhelpful or helpful, escapist or healthy escape. Return for a moment to Cavell and skepticism. Suppose someone really did experience solipsism, rather than just believing that what it means is right. Suppose further that this cast him into the depths of despond. Deflecting his problem by turning it into philosophical debate might be the best possible way out of his difficulty—escapism, but an escape to better health. A deeper deflection, perhaps Wittgenstein's at various times in his life, might be better, and certainly would be better philosophy, but we cannot all be the best of philosophers.

Diamond believes that philosophizing about animals deflects reality in a way that she thinks is pernicious. It is well to put beside that the fact that Peter Singer is the most influential living philosopher. I do not mean that he is the most important or that he has a great influence on philosophers. I mean that he has influenced more people than any other philosopher alive. Ever since 1973 he has been the intellectual leader of movements for animal liberation and rights.[9] His first book on animal liberation sold half a million copies. Costello and Diamond think that his arguments miss the main points; perhaps that explains, at a deep level, why I, at a surface level, do not think they are logically compelling.

Singer starts with the claim that animals have interests because they are sentient, capable of pain and pleasure. When I reflect on my own actions and responses, I see that I occasionally do something good for some other people who are far from my circle of friends, family, or even countrymen, and perhaps beyond the call of any common duty. But I do not do so because they have interests or because I respect their interests or because they are sentient—nor because they have rights. I often do not understand why I do it. It is partly what I have been trained to do, and childhood training does not readily wear off. It is also something else, a certain kind of sharing, of sympathy between myself and another, what Hume claimed was the basis of moral action. So say I; but it is Singer's invocation of rights that persuades people.

The place of Singer's reasons may be more forensic than moral. We need codes and precedents to regulate civil society. Singer and his fellows are forging the laws of tomorrow. Laws have moral stature not only because they create legal duties and obligations but also because they are benchmarks from which to move on. Grandin's norm for abattoirs has the same virtue.

Singer does present arguments, but they should be filed under the heading of rhetoric, not logic. Some misreading of Aristotle has conned American colleges into teaching symbolic logic to all and humane rhetoric to none. Rhetoric matters. I doubt that Diamond, Cavell, or McDowell undervalues the influence of Singer, even though theirs is a different way in which to practice the philosophical arts. I am not disagreeing with them in what I have said, nor do I disagree with Diamond that Singer deflects from reality. I am repeating myself: Don't knock deflection.

ASTONISHMENT AND AWE

Czeslaw Milosz demands that we be astonished at the very existence of beauty—awed by it. "It should not exist." Ruth Klüger insists that the act of a woman in Auschwitz who so meaningfully helped her when she was a terrified child should fill us with astonishment and awe.

Diamond writes, "Instances of goodness or of beauty can throw us. . . . we cannot fit it into the understanding we have of what the world is like." She includes this experience among the difficulties of reality. I shall seem an ungracious philistine by asking why it is a difficulty of reality.

It may be that philosophers speaking the language of principles, propositions, and arguments cannot fit awe in the face of beauty into their discourse. Perhaps that is a difficulty of philosophy. Poets do not make sense of beauty either. They do not fit it into the understanding of what the world is like. Need that matter? We do not have to follow Plato and cast our lot only with philosophers to the exclusion of poets, and I am sure that Diamond would not want us to.

The following well-known lines express something important.

> For Beauty's nothing
> but beginning of terror we're just able to bear,
> and why we adore it so is because it serenely
> disdains to destroy us.[10]

I dislike Rilke's evident sense of his own self-importance. To use Diamond's paraphrasing of Milosz, I prefer the humility of "the mystery that may seem to be present in the architecture of a tree, the slimness of a column crowned with green." This mystery *is* part of my reality, perhaps just because it is not fittable into the world as I understand it. Rilke's awe is fitting. The fact that we cannot talk it and can at best quote Rilke is less a difficulty of reality than part of it.

It is true that philosophers want to express very clearly in well-understood words *everything* that is to be experienced. Rilke had something to say about saying, in a less well known poem published in 1908. "Der Einsame" ("The Solitary Man") begins as follows:

> No, what my heart will be is a tower,
> And I will be right on its rim
> Nothing else will be there, only pain
> And what can't be said, only the world.[11]

The solitary, as opposed to the dependent, man is also mentioned in the fourth of Rilke's *Letters to a Young Poet* (16 July 1903). Unsayability is there qualified with an "almost," which, to a philosophical mind, seems wise. Speaking of complex emotions of love and sex, Rilke says that "even the most articulate people are unable to help, since what words point to is so very delicate, is almost unsayable."

GRACE

Diamond continues by introducing Ruth Klüger. Goodness presses in upon us, not as with Hughes or Costello, with pointless death or selfish indifference to wanton cruelty. Certainly we deflect the intense awareness of good if we take it for granted, if we recite a sort of banality of goodness: by a shrug, OK, some persons are altruistic, no surprise in that. "Here, as in the case of the Hughes poem," writes Diamond, "what is capable of astonishing one is its incomprehensibility." Is that the right word? Why should we be astonished that there is so much in the world that we do not comprehend? Can we not be *simply* filled with wonder, with the apprehension of what Klüger calls grace?

Of course, Diamond must agree. Her point is that we cannot comprehend it by "taking it apart." We must see whole, and not deflect with analysis. Diamond the philosopher is making us stop and experience what we might have passed by. As philosopher, she is restoring her readers' capacity to experience unanalyzed wonder, to make goodness and beauty awe-full again.

THE DANGER OF TOO MUCH LANGUAGE

McDowell offers a diagnosis of the difficulty of reality, by way of an account of what so deeply troubles Elizabeth Costello.[12] Alluding to both Hughes's poem and to Coetzee's lectures, he writes:

> The kind of difficulty both cases exemplify arises when something we encounter defeats our ordinary capacity to get our minds around reality, that is, our capacity to capture reality in language. That dislodges us from comfortably inhabiting our nature as speaking animals, animals who make sense of things in the way the capacity to speak enables us. The special kind of animal life we lead comes into question.   (134)

The difficulty will be even greater for Costello, the novelist whose life work is words. This is a very complex thought, which many will find helpful, in thinking through Diamond's essay. Nevertheless it seems to me to overplay the importance of saying in a way that Diamond does not.

Notoriously, philosophers who characterize Man as the Talking Animal have gone on to draw consequences for the ways in which we ought to relate to nonspeaking animals. McDowell does no such thing. He does not define Man as a creature whose nature it is to speak, but his words may still invite the thought that speaking, above all, is what makes people special, the "special kind of animal life we lead."

He uses the two phrases to characterize one and the same capacity, namely, "our capacity to capture reality in language" and "our ordinary capacity to get our minds around reality." The former too much recalls Cavell's animadversions on "clutching," to which Diamond alludes. And although "getting my mind around reality" sounds lovely as metaphor, it may not be a philosophically felicitous way to describe an "ordinary capacity" of "ours."

As a precautionary note, we should record that Temple Grandin would certainly protest, if she were willing to talk this way, that she gets her mind around many important aspects of reality just because she does not think in words. What we call her disability is compensated by other abilities, a theme now popular in what may be called the autism liberation front. I do not, however, wish to lay emphasis on abilities that "we" may take to be grounded in pathologies.

Here is an ordinary, personal fact. As I write this summer, I am privileged, here on a hillside, looking out on tall pines that grow out of the earth far below me. When I look straight ahead over my computer monitor, I see them halfway up, at the top of their bare trunks, and just before their crown begins. This is an extraordinarily beautiful and peaceful sight. It is also alive, varying, because often the clouds rise to this level, and the trees are wraithed in mist.

There: I have just given you some idea of the vista I am so blessed as to have before me. I cannot possibly "capture this reality in language." I am not thereby dislodged from comfortably inhabiting my nature as a speaking animal because other aspects of my nature are far more involved in what I experience, now, than is my ability to describe.

You can see why, in this setting, I resonated with Milosz on trees. You may also see why the metaphor of getting my mind around reality did not help. It simply does not *connect*. As I pause and look out again, I ask, do I get my mind around *this* reality before me? If that means to *possess* it, of course not, the very thought is insulting. But when I will myself to talk this way, it does seem to me that, as I sit here, my mind is around this reality (if that means anything at all). I am almost literally on the rim of a tower, for a moment solitary, with "what can't be said, only the world."

McDowell is referring not to something serene but to Hughes's 1914 reality and Costello's "putative" reality. Nevertheless, I have been making use of the third in Diamond's series of examples, so what I have just said is relevant. The analogies do seem to carry through. On reading Hughes's poem I get my mind around the lousy reality (if that means anything at all). I stopped short with his other poem, "Out," partly because my capacity to speak about its reality had to be actively stopped. It will be said that I totally miss McDowell's point.

I began by quoting Costello. She spoke of "philosophical language." Perhaps for a moment she would allow McDowell to speak for her. If so, she might say that philosophical language does not "capture" the reality of animal life that she experiences. Indeed, nothing can fully capture it. But her words, both philosophical and nonphilosophical, in the course of both her lectures, certainly say a lot about it. With Cora Diamond we may come to think that the propositions, principles, and arguments of animal rights discourse deflect reality but that Costello, the novelist, has other resources.

NOTES

1. For references, see the notes to Cary Wolfe's introduction.

2. I was brought in to this discussion only because I wrote one of the first long reviews of Coetzee's Tanner Lectures (*The New York Review of Books*, 29 June 2000, 20–26), and a follow-up, "On Sympathy: With Other Living Creatures," *Tijdschrift voor Filosofie* 63 (2001): 683–712. A few lines from the review are repeated in the present comments.

3. J. M. Coetzee, *Boyhood: Scenes from Provincial Life* (London: Secker and Warburg, 1997), 1–2.

4. Except in Canada, whose Supreme Court ruled for the Patent Office and against Harvard, so that oncomice and their ilk cannot be patented in Canada. (Patent laws, for historical reasons of precedent, are surprisingly different in neighboring common-law jurisdictions.) One argument before the court was that once altered, oncomice breed just like mice, and so cannot be patented. An argument for allowing turkeys to be patented? The question of breeding monsters was not introduced in court, only that of patenting life forms which, once generated, can regenerate themselves.

5. Temple Grandin and Catherine Johnson, *Animals in Translation: Using the Mysteries of Autism to Decode Animal Behavior* (New York: Scribner, 2005).

6. J. M. Coetzee, *Disgrace* (London: Secker and Warburg, 1999), 217.

7. Reviel Netz, *Barbed Wire: An Ecology of Modernity* (Middletown, Conn.: Wesleyan University Press, 2004).

8. "Ted Hughes at the Adelaide Festival Writers' Week, March 1976," http://www.zeta.org.au/~annskea/Adelaide.htm.

9. Starting with his article in the *New York Review of Books*, 5 April 1973, followed in 1975 by *Animal Liberation: A New Ethics for our Treatment of Animals*, 2nd ed. (New York: New York Review/Random House, 1990).

10. Ranier Maria Rilke, "The First Elegy," in *The Duino Elegies*, trans. J. B. Leishman and Stephen Spender (London: The Hogarth Press, 1957), lines 4–7.

11. Poem 87 of 96 in *New Poems*, trans. J. B. Leishman (London: The Hogarth Press, 1964). "Nein: ein Turm soll sein aus meinem Herzen / und ich selbst an seinen Rand gestellt: / wo sonst nichts mehr ist, noch einmal Schmerzen / und Unsäglichkeit, noch einmal Welt" (in *Der neuen Gedichte Anderer Teil* [Munich: Insel Verlag, 1908]).

12. The expression "too much language" in the subhead is from Bertold Brecht, precisely in making rude remarks about Descartes. See the second of my "Five Parables," in *Philosophy in Its Context*, ed. R. Rorty, J. Schneewind, and Q. Skinner (Cambridge: Cambridge University Press, 1984), 103–24.

It is not something about our pets that keeps us from eating them, but rather something about ourselves, about our need for or reliance on or enjoyment of companions